Project Management in the Ed Tech Era

In the Education Technology planning and project management field, methods have been developed that help mitigate Ed Tech and IT project failures—that is, strategic planning and project management.

The MAPIT® series of two books covers these areas in order of execution:

1. *FAIL TO PLAN, PLAN TO FAIL: How to Develop Your School's Education Technology Strategic Plan*, is focused on Strategic Technology Plan development.

2. *PROJECT MANAGEMENT IN THE ED TECH ERA: How to Successfully Plan and Manage Your School's Next Innovation*, is focused on tactical project planning and the practice and methods of project management.

Project Management in the Ed Tech Era

How to Successfully Plan and Manage Your School's Next Innovation

Darryl Vidal

ROWMAN & LITTLEFIELD
Lanham • Boulder • New York • London

Published by Rowman & Littlefield
A wholly owned subsidiary of The Rowman & Littlefield Publishing Group, Inc.
4501 Forbes Boulevard, Suite 200, Lanham, Maryland 20706
www.rowman.com

Unit A, Whitacre Mews, 26–34 Stannary Street, London SE11 4AB

Copyright © 2018 by Darryl Vidal

All rights reserved. No part of this book may be reproduced in any form or by any electronic or mechanical means, including information storage and retrieval systems, without written permission from the publisher, except by a reviewer who may quote passages in a review.

British Library Cataloguing-in-Publication Information Available

Library of Congress Cataloging-in-Publication Data Available

ISBN 978-1-4758-3547-2 (cloth : alk. paper)
ISBN 978-1-4758-3548-9 (pbk. alk. paper)
ISBN 978-1-4758-3549-6 (electronic)

Contents

Foreword		vii
Preface		xi
Introduction		xiii
MAPIT® IT Project Management		xiii
Strategic Planning versus Project Planning		xiii
1	**Project Fundamentals**	**1**
	Project Plan	2
	Project Management	2
	Key Concepts	13
	First Things First: Project Initiation	19
2	**Core Processes: Creating the Project Plan**	**27**
	Scope Development	30
	Task Definitions	40
	Task Sequencing	49
	Resource Staffing	56
	Schedule Development	59
	Project Budget	64
	Plan Development	70
3	**Support Processes**	**77**
	Communications Plan	79
	Project Control Plan	81
	Resource Staffing Plan	85
	Risk Management Plan	87

Change Management Plan	94
Quality Assurance Plan	97
Data Integrity Plan	101
Project Completion, Acceptance, Delivery, and Closeout	103
Project Execution	107
Final Thoughts	**109**
Project Management is the Project Manager	109
About the Author	**111**

Foreword

For the past three decades, our society has struggled with the explosion of computers, digital devices, smartphones, and extreme changes in how we communicate. For school administrators, it wasn't enough to just manage the complexities of academia, school finance, and collective bargaining. These brave souls had to discover, acquire, and eventually plan for this technology while the landscape around them constantly shifted and reformed. All of this was necessary even while our society and the students morphed into something almost unrecognizable from previous generations.

As a K–12 superintendent for three school districts over a 19-year period and as a 30-year educator, I have seen it all. I lived through this "explosive" period of time but not unscathed. We didn't start with a capacity for strategic planning; we just tried to be good at operations and "just in time" management. We were most concerned with "making things right" rather than "making the right things" and taking the time to chart a course for success.

We saw the general notion of planning in schools as being budgeting and scheduling, short-range planning such as recruitment and program modifications, and then finally long-range planning, albeit most of us were not performing this latter task. We knew change was happening; we just couldn't ever seem to get ahead of it. Something was different about this change movement.

What was different about this change was the speed of the change. Monumental changes occurred over a short period of time causing a cultural upheaval unheard of in human history. Business has changed, governments are changing, cultures have changed, and people are drastically changing how they interrelate with one another and how they communicate with one another. It is undeniable then that the learner and our schools have changed and are changing. It is for this reason that those in educational leadership roles became agents for change and attempted to plan appropriately.

Society moved from the slower pace and relative stability of the twentieth century to the fluid, fast-paced, and relentlessly changing twenty-first century. We now live in an era of interconnected economies and integrated technologies, which create constant tension in our lives and force rapid changes to our culture. The introduction of technology in a school meant that administrators had to become knowledgeable about broadband, Ethernet, and dark fiber. They quickly became advocates for the increased use of one-to-one laptops, Bring Your Own Device (BYOD), pervasive Wi-Fi, learning management systems, and open educational resources. On the fly research was snatched the minute it was published giving the school leaders research-based permission to make transformational change in their schools.

There are three tasks school administrators must undertake in order to prepare the pathway for transformation in their school or district. First, they must change their paradigm of how schools operate, their attitude toward instructional methods and the personalization of learning, and how the use of educational technology can promote these changes. Second, knowing that a paradigm shift has occurred, they must retrain instructors. Professional development is vital to keeping pace with the today's unique cultural dynamic. And third, they must understand the importance of proper planning in order to implement a robust, application-rich infrastructure that is systemic, sustainable, and capable of future growth.

Darryl Vidal's primary instructional focus for the past two decades has been the ever-evolving use of technology in K–12 classrooms. Darryl's new book continues to expand on his unique formal strategic planning and project management methodology known as MAPIT®. He utilizes this book to make school leaders be more familiar with the "triple constraint" element to any functional strategic plan of scope, time, and budget. He fully recognizes how imperative it is for a school district to plan and implement a strong technology infrastructure that provides for an unsure future of continued growth and change and uses his expertise to clearly inform the education community.

This second book of the MAPIT® Project Management series focuses on the project manager as the key to the success of the management of a project. Darryl Vidal elevates the project manager to the rightful position of kingpin for proper implementation. As the cornerstone to the project, the project manager must use all of his or her skills necessary to achieve victory for the organization. This book provides in detail the skills needed for success, how to acquire those skills, and most important, when to use them for maximum effectiveness.

I hope you enjoy reading this book as much as I have and that you acquire the additional knowledge you will need to successfully manage any size of school or district. We could have used this book back in the 90s; now you can take advantage of this wisdom for tomorrow's children.

Jeffrey P. Felix, EdD
Retired superintendent/educational technology consultant

Preface

In over 20 years working with schools delivering state-of-the-art technology systems, from infrastructure to integration to classroom technology, there is always the project and the plan. We need only to look at your most recent education technology project and ask, "Is it a success?" Which of course will beg the question what do we consider success?

Obviously, in the greater scheme of things education-wise, success must be based on student outcomes. But there are many underlying metrics that can also be used to measure success for more practical and pragmatic reasons. As an information technology consultant working in K–12 education, we're always looking at decision making from a justification standpoint—each dollar spent must support an educational objective. But in an education technology realm with speeds, feeds, bandwidth, and operating systems, how do we measure educational technology effectiveness? And to take a more proactive approach, how do we insure educational technology effectiveness?

In the past decades of innovative technology initiatives, true successes resulting in higher test scores and/or higher college acceptance levels have not carried the headlines. Blogging, learning management system (LMS), podcasting, flipping, one-to-one, and BYOD have brought many examples of pilot successes and case studies, but the point of this book is not to help you identify and create the next technology innovation. The point of this book is to help you actually plan and successfully deliver your school's technology innovation.

This book is about execution—delivering on a plan. But that assumes you're already three to four steps down a path. A path that began with a VISION, which became a STRATEGY, which bore out INITIATIVES, which required SYSTEMS, some of which required TECHNOLOGIES. If you aren't fully conversant on these preceding phases, check out the other books I've written which address each of these:

- *VISION: The First Critical Step in Developing a Strategy for Education Technology* and
- *FAIL TO PLAN, PLAN TO FAIL: How to Create Your School's Education Technology Strategic Plan*

Technology initiatives are not pet projects, pilots, or proofs of concept. Strategic technology plans must be developed at the school-district level to fully understand near-term and longer-term initiatives based on academic objectives. Once these strategies and initiatives are identified and prioritized, that's when project planning comes to the fore.

EVERY PROJECT NEEDS PLANNING: THE QUESTIONS ARE *HOW* AND *HOW MUCH*?

This book provides the most streamlined methods for defining, developing, documenting, and executing any education technology project. It provides the methods to insure integrity and accuracy in the planning phase and control and communication in the execution phase. It defines how projects start and end and all the milestones and control points in the middle. And it details how you can execute it all.

After reading this book, you will have the methods, templates, and examples, in order to deliver successful education technology projects, but more important, this book will give you the insights of how to become a successful education technology project manager.

Introduction

MAPIT® IT PROJECT MANAGEMENT

More than 80% of technology projects fail! What does that mean? In planning and project management parlance, it means the project has broken one of the three constraints (a.k.a. triple constraint): scope, time, and budget. These three factors hold the key to a functional strategic plan, and their subsequent implementation plans, to define the successful education technology project.

If you've picked up this book, that might mean you've already read *FAIL TO PLAN, PLAN TO FAIL: How to Create Your School's Education Technology Strategic Plan*, a book specifically about MAPIT® strategic technology planning. That doesn't mean you must go back and read that one first; this book stands alone as a project planning and project management primer based on MAPIT® project planning and project management.

The first book in this series provides a method for strategic technology planning for K–20 educational institutions. This book is focused on project planning and project management of IT projects in the education realm. One might wonder, what's the difference between strategic planning and project planning besides the semantics and scope. So let's define them.

STRATEGIC PLANNING VERSUS PROJECT PLANNING

Education technology strategic planning attempts to put an umbrella over all of a school's technology initiatives to define and develop objectives that insure that all technology initiatives are based on academic goals and curricular needs. Project planning encompasses the scope of a specific project. This specific project might be a subproject of a larger initiative, or it might be a project all itself. Either way, its scope is limited to the tactical objective, whereas the strategic technology plan attempts to arrange, prioritize, and organize all technology initiatives to accomplish an overall technology vision.

To implement a strategic plan, one must execute tactical plans. The individual tactical plans are not necessarily technology projects because they might easily be facilities or infrastructure projects required to support a technology program. For instance, upgrading all the power services to a school site to support new network equipment would be an electrical upgrade as a subproject to a network upgrade. Doing a large furniture procurement for classrooms might be a subproject to a large-scale technology modernization project, but all these projects and subprojects will require a project plan.

The goals and objectives of a strategic technology plan are to provide a high-level road map that will organize and prioritize initiatives or projects in order to communicate and accomplish a long-range vision. The priorities in a strategic plan are based on bottom-up infrastructure requirements, funding availability, and classroom/student impact. The strategic planning process should provide rough-order magnitude (ROM) cost models that allow the planner to assemble the initiatives accordingly for balanced impact throughout the school.

The goals and objectives of a project plan are to define the project in very specific terms, define and organize the tasks, plan and engage resources, and the most important metrics of a project, start and complete it. The projects are prioritized based on the strategic plan, and then it is contingent upon the leadership to endorse the project planning process, as well as provide leadership (a project manager) and resources (money) to plan and execute the project.

The strategic plan should provide a generalized timescale (duration) and implementation timeline (project duration within the overall strategy), while the project plan will attempt to start and complete the project within the timeline window. Whereas a strategic technology plan may not have a specified end date, a project must have a completion, commissioning, and due date. This may be the most important difference between strategic plans and project plans—if a project doesn't end, it's not a project—it's a quagmire.

This is where the project's success is measured. Where a strategic technology plan is for all in an organization to know and understand, the project plan is for the project manager (PM), his or her clients, and resources. No one else needs to be involved. As long as the project is delivered on time and on budget, high-level stakeholders may not need to be involved.

Chapter 2—"Core Processes"—comprises the process and methods for developing a project plan and all its components, including designs, budgets, and timelines. Chapter 3—"Support Processes"—comprises the plans and methods to manage and control the execution phase of the project. Together, these comprise the MAPIT® project planning and project management methodologies.

Chapter 1

Project Fundamentals

Let's start with some definitions:

What is a project?

- "A planned set of interrelated tasks to be executed over a fixed period and within certain cost and other limitations" (Business Dictionary).
- "A project is temporary in that it has a defined beginning and end in time, and therefore defined scope and resources" (Project Management Institute).

What is project management?

- "The application of processes, methods, knowledge, skills and experience to achieve the project objectives" (Project Management Institute).
- "The discipline of initiating, planning, executing, controlling, and closing the work of a team to achieve specific goals and meet specific success criteria" (Wikipedia).

What is the triple constraint?

- "The combination of the three most significant restrictions on any project: scope, schedule and cost" (TechTarget).
- We only need one definition for this one.

What is a project plan?

- Different from a strategic plan, a project plan details the tasks of a project, its durations, and interdependencies.
- A project plan defines resources and durations for each task.

PROJECT PLAN

This book is divided into two major components, project planning (Core Processes) and project management (Support Processes). Even though the first book in this series was about strategic planning, almost none of that planning process applies to project planning.

The first part of any project is the planning process, but there's actually a phase before it. Without it the project cannot start. It is the project initiation phase. Project initiation is all the things that must happen for a project to begin. Likely there are proposals, quotations, bids, and estimates.

Invariably, in order to engage a company or firm, there must be a signed contract or purchase order. In larger procurements there must be requests for proposals (RFPs), notices to proceed (NTPs), and board approvals. All these things are part of project initiation, and if the project manager (PM) is on board at this stage of the project, he or she should be aware that nothing starts without initial engagement vehicles.

Every project must have the following phases:

1. Project initiation
2. Project plan development
3. Project execution
4. Project completion

Each of these phases may have as many as 10 to 20 tasks and subtasks. Figure 1.1—"Project Phases"—illustrates the sequence and dependencies of the project phases.

PROJECT MANAGEMENT

Project management may be one of the most overused and misused terms in the English language, coming in close behind systems and solutions. But unlike systems and solutions, project management denotes a human component—the PM. It is implicitly understood that project management requires a PM.

Despite all efforts to automate, control, and standardize processes, project management will never be a process or service that is performed without a human resource component. But not only does project management require human intervention, it also requires tasks and deliverables, the respective definition of these as well as knowledge of the objective results.

Unlike the landscaper who can cut the grass and trim the trees, the PM must render his or her services along with many objective and subjective

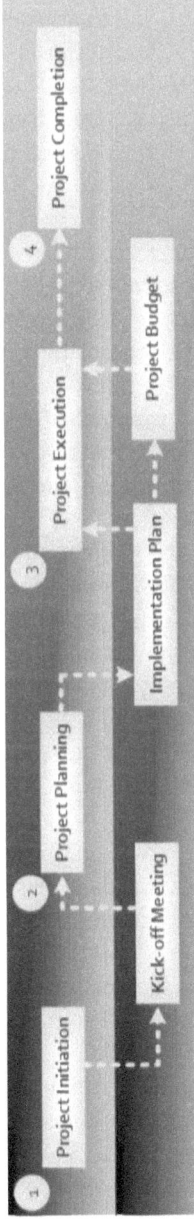

Project Phases

Figure 1.1 Project Phases

deliverables. What are subjective deliverables? Concepts like customer satisfaction, data integrity, project control, and risk mitigation are all components of a successful project that are subjective but still concrete measures of success. In fact, it may be surmised that project management consists of the following: people, processes, attitude, accountability, and documentation. Although it's quite simple to assemble a list of resources, requirements, and skills required to be a PM, these are key, and they include very specific context when used within the realm of projects and project management.

People

Unlike many other products and services, project management (and project planning as a component) is inherently people oriented. Just on the surface we can immediately identify additional parties beyond the PM. Of course, there is the client. In education this would likely be at the district level a director of IT or, at the very minimum, a principal of a school with a large project. Other clients may include facilities managers, assistant superintendents and superintendents, and of course our end-all clients in education, the students and teachers.

Beyond direct participants in the project who are likely the IT director or the facilities director, and the PM, there are usually a cast of supporting project resources such as vendor PMs, vendor technical staff, manufacturer account managers, and technical staff as well as contractors and their PMs and technical staff. Each of these players in the project(s) will be responsible for his or her scope of the project, and the players often must limit their involvement in the project as much as possible because their immediate responsibilities are to their clients, of whom, the school is one, but not the only one.

Interestingly enough, no matter how large the system and procurement, the manufacturer's account manager still usually has a monthly or quarterly goal that demands their attention and resources beyond their current client's projects. In fact, from the manufacturer's standpoint, once the equipment is sold, the manufacturer is looking to the systems integrator or value-added reseller (VAR) as accountable for the successful implementation of the project and objectives.

Similarly, vendors, contractors, and system integrators typically will have their assigned PMs, who must manage resources and coordinate with the end client for their own project success. As a designee of the district and director, the PM becomes the only resource directly responsible for the project success. The PM becomes an abstraction layer between the project and the school to provide a single point of contact and ultimate accountability for the project.

The point being made here is that project management is about the PM. His or her ability to plan, manage, and coordinate resources is the critical success factor. The PM steps up to the table to accept and be accountable to the success of the project but in doing so also demands the respect and support of those critical resources. In fact, it is best to understand that project management *is the project manager*!

Stakeholders

Stakeholders are typically the beneficiaries of the project but also may include interested parties who have some level of authority or reliance upon the success of the subject project. For instance, the school district leadership, above and around the IT director, are stakeholders, just as the board of education. But also the students and their parents (taxpayers) are stakeholders. In fact, oftentimes, taxpayers who are no longer parents of school-age children may be the most vocal stakeholders the PM may be concerned with.

The PM must take the opportunity to define the stakeholders in coordination with the client. The PM must never assume a person who has interaction with the project is not a stakeholder for it is at his or her peril that he or she makes a communication and neglects to include that stakeholder. The PM will discover quickly and not so discretely that he or she has ignored an important stakeholder. Regarding stakeholder communications, it's always safer to include and be instructed to exclude than vice versa.

Since IT systems tend to impact all factions of school operations and curriculum in today's educational environment, it is hard to think of someone connected to the school who is not a stakeholder, especially if the project is some sort of IT infrastructure project like 10Gbps core networking or VoIP implementation. Even systems such as learning management systems (LMSs), cybersecurity, and electronic mail (e-mail) are considered infrastructure. Even though projectors and telephones aren't often considered IT systems, they are, and people rely on them more and more, to the point where their failure directly impacts classroom productivity and, of course, student learning. When was the last time the wireless network failed and multiple classrooms and teachers could not perform their scheduled curriculum activities?

In the old days, if the computers failed, the teacher simply took out the paper and textbooks, but in today's fully integrated technology classroom and school, an infrastructure or cloud-based resource failure could render the school district totally crippled both from an operations and an academic standpoint. Loss of a firewall for the whole district would not only take out the Internet connectivity, but along with it cloud-based services (student information system, LMSs, or County Office of Education personnel or budget applications) would bring all of school productivity to a halt. So stakeholders abound, but the PM as taskmaster is not sufficient. The PM must support himself or herself and his or her project with processes.

Processes

Processes are the workflows, decision points, actions, and engagement that move a project from kick-off through hand-off. Processes support planning and management of all parts of a project, including scope development, task definition, sequencing, staffing scheduling, budgeting, and execution. These may be discrete plans or parts of an overall project plan. More important, processes support the PM. By providing the PM with the structure, and sequence, all resources must commit their scope of capability and responsibility, their availability, and their commitment to execution within a time frame. This is a key part of the planning process.

Processes also are a tool of the PM to leverage and account for tasks and their delivery times. By elevating the project to the highest priority, the PM utilizes the processes to evoke the resources to either perform or proclaim their inability to perform so the PM can look to other resources. By relying on these processes on a regular frequency, the resources know their scope of responsibility, when their tasks are due, and that they must report their progress on this basis.

One of the greatest resources of the PM is the standing weekly status meeting. This is where all current task resources must meet and discuss the status and readiness for upcoming tasks. By taking responsibility of the project tasks, the project resources become the staff of the PM. The PM needs to only ask about the status of tasks, and the resources must bring to bear the reality of their situation. No undue or extraneous pressure needs to be applied by the PM. Through the project management section of this book, we will discuss all the tools and plans available to the PM to help define, secure, and hold accountable all resources and stakeholders.

Attitude

Although the PM's attitude is a much more subjective aspect of project management, it becomes an important method and technique enabling the PM to disassociate himself or herself from the pressure of task accountability and project risk. The PM should be able to manage a project with no emotion but the effort to deliver the plan on time and on budget.

By engaging resources under the need for progress to project milestones, the PM exerts the pressure of the overall objective and simply becomes the messenger of the project need. At the same time the PM must not exert overt pressure on resources and rather have the resources report progress and risks. By allowing resources to proclaim risks, they in turn must address factors to mitigate those risks. Thereby the PM's attitude becomes like the following: What's going on? Why are you putting the whole project at risk? What can be done to keep the project on schedule?

PM Perspective

Occasionally, PM perspectives will be included to help editorialize the concepts and ideas about attitude and disposition that will benefit the PM. Keep in mind the PM has the project on his or her side. As long as all his or her insistence to adhere to due dates, and hold resources accountable, is in advocation of the project, he or she is in the right. If his or her attitude or temper moves outside the bounds of scope, time, and budget, then the PM loses credibility and becomes a creature not of the project but outside of the project.

The PM cannot allow personality to dictate behavior. His effort is to make the project successful and his clients look good. The project is never about the PM. The PM should never point fingers, assign blame, or defend himself or herself.

Accountability

Accountability may be one of the most difficult aspects of a project to enforce, but the PM has the duty to do his or her best to uphold accountability of resources in the effort to deliver a project on time and on budget. Accountability means different things to different resources of the project. Let's look at some examples in the following table; we can view a resource, their connection to a project, and their level of accountability. Table 1.1—"Accountability Matrix"—provides examples of the PM's ability to enforce accountability with project resources, and the risk the PM is exposed to if the resource does not comply.

Although the table may make it look like district staff is more or less immune to accountability, this is not entirely true. Even though we would not hope an IT director or facilities manager would lose his or her job over a technology program, the project controls certainly could provide the documentation that identifies which resources are missing the mark. If the PM publishes a risk report that identifies lack of progress by an internal department, the PM would have to rely on district leadership to apply pressure and enforce accountability within their organization.

Table 1.1 Accountability Matrix

Resource	Relationship	Enforcement	Risk
Project manager	Agent to school	Disengagement	Project failure
Facilities manager	School manager	Reporting / risk	Task failure
IT director	PM supervisor	Reporting to leadership	Project delay/failure
Manufacturer	Equipment	Replacement	Project delay
Vendor/integrator	Contract service provider	Disengagement penalty	Project delay/failure
Contractor	Contract provider	Disengagement damages	Project delay/failure

The salient point in this discussion is that the PM must understand the accountability context for each project resource. If he or she can anticipate an uncooperative internal resource, weekly status reporting and project control documentation (chapter 3) will be the key to keeping these resources accountable. That's not to say that vendors, contractors, and manufacturers can't be held accountable; they are all at risk of being fired. Of course, we know that replacement of formally engaged resources is also not that simple. This is why the processes and documentation must be adhered to and enforced.

Escalation

Escalation must be viewed as a necessary evil of project management. Escalation is the remediation activity tied to accountability. The objective of escalation is not as a punishment as a form of accountability but a remediation effort—to not have to enforce or punish. However, if the escalation or remediation does not result in the intended outcome, the escalation should also have a punishment or implication of subversion.

The fact that escalation must occur is triggered by a resource not performing as required by the project. The PM must be disciplined about first, anticipating escalation, mitigation of the need for escalation, and if all else fails taking remediation actions in escalation.

Mitigation of escalation means that the PM has taken an action to communicate the urgency of a task with the responsible resource in effort to NOT miss a deadline. Take note that this mitigation must occur BEFORE a deadline or due date has been missed. That likely means that the Level 1 escalation should happen in a reasonable amount of time before the Level 2 escalation occurs. If the PM doesn't warn the resource of the impending missed due date, then the PM is guilty of not communicating this task's due date effectively—not managing the project effectively. It directly means that Level 1 escalation must occur several days before the task's due date and that the Level 2 escalation should go out to its distribution list also before the missed due date. If these escalations don't occur before the missed due date, then the PM is simply reporting project delays after the fact—a failure of the time constraint.

Figure 1.2—"Escalation Procedure"—provides a graphic representation of the timing of escalation actions. The important factor in this escalation model is the anticipation of a missed due date. This would also typically trigger a risk assessment and possibly the change management process. It is not acceptable to escalate a project delay after the fact. This is just a report of project impact and rescheduling of resources and activities. The escalation activities must precede a missed task due date.

Does this mean that the PM must have extrasensory perception? Kind of. It does mean that the PM must be fully aware of the project timeline and related activities. He or she must have enough knowledge of the activity and implementation to begin to anticipate if due dates continue to be realistic as the project progresses. Although the graphic depicts escalation activities starting two weeks prior to a possible missed due date, this timescale is specific to each task. For instance, if construction of a new facility is going to take four months, and four months out from the due date, a contractor has not been awarded a contract, escalation activities must begin at least two months before the task START date in order to complete within months of the planned completion date.

Escalation should have at least three levels:

- Level 1: Notice of possible missed due date and risk assessment report
- Level 2: Notice of pending missed due date and risk mitigation and/or change management report
- Level 3: Notice of missed due date and change management process

Table 1.2—"Escalation Matrix"—provides a matrix of possible actions to escalate priority of tasks required of project resources.

PM Perspective

How can the PM enforce accountability with district internal resources without making enemies of those resources? Consider the context and means of attempted enforcement. If an internal resource such as the network engineer within the district IT department is not available to support the system integrator, the method of enforcement would be e-mail requests for status that

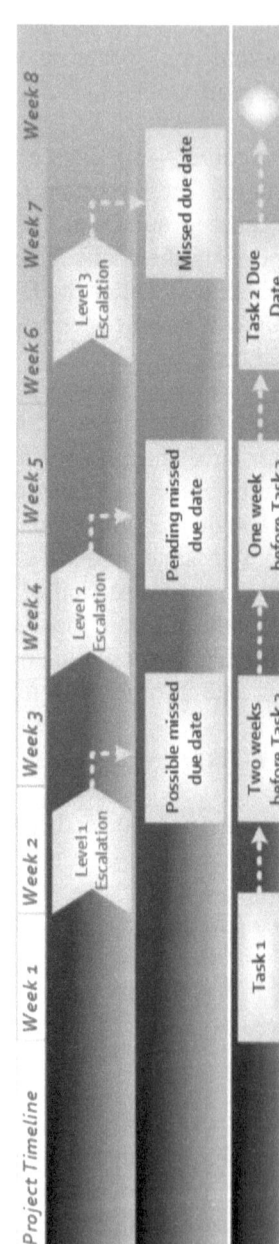

Figure 1.2 Escalation Procedure

Table 1.2 Escalation Matrix

Resource	Level 1	Level 2	Level 3
Internal staff (not IT)	E-mail request for tasks by due date and risk assessment	Second e-mail request with supervisor and IT director copied and risk mitigation	Change management triggered and submitted to leadership
IT staff	E-mail request for tasks by due date and risk assessment	Second e-mail request with IT director copied and risk mitigation	Change management triggered and submitted to leadership
Facilities manager	E-mail request for tasks by due date and risk assessment	Second e-mail request with district leadership copied and risk mitigation	Change management triggered and submitted to leadership
IT director	E-mail request for tasks by due date and risk assessment	Second e-mail request with district leadership copied and risk mitigation	Change management triggered and submitted to leadership
Vendor/ integrator	E-mail to vendor PM and account manager and risk assessment	Second e-mail request with district leadership and vendor executives and risk mitigation	Change management triggered and/or actions to district leadership
Contractor	E-mail to contractor PM and account manager and risk assessment	Second e-mail request with district leadership and contractor executives and risk mitigation	Change management triggered and/or actions to district leadership

include escalating the level of management that are copied on the requests and issuance of risk assessment reports. Once again, if these requests do not begin before the missed due dates, the blame will shift from the resource to the PM.

Documentation

Documentation is the archive of action. Documentation is proof of delivery. In project planning and project management, documentation is the deliverable that substantiates the product. If the project is to provide Wi-Fi saturation to a school site, then the deliverables are the working Wi-Fi network AND the documentation that supports it. The accounts payable department cannot pay the integrator for a Wi-Fi network without a documented acknowledgment by the client/stakeholder—and it's a piece of paper (or an electronic document).

In fact, there should be a plethora of supporting documentation for any project beginning at the initial planning stages, through weekly status reporting, change management and risk management reports, punch list verification, system documentation, verification testing documentation, and final commissioning report. There are also bills of material, invoices, equipment lists, asset inventory lists, architectural drawings, and floor plans. That is to say these documents are being created, whether formally or informally, and the only reason there would be no supporting documentation for any particular project would be the PM's own negligence to capture and publish this deliverable. The documentation and its acceptance by the stakeholder provide the milestone for final project completion and payment.

In a software implementation project, lacking physical plans and AS-BUILT drawings, there still should be scopes of work, product lists, licensing documents, maintenance and support contracts, configuration listings, and of course, user manuals and systems documentation.

Alternately, documentation can be a pile of senseless chaos. If the PM took this variety of lists, data, and drawings, and put them in a binder without a table of contents, a logical description and explanation of the sections, the deliverable would provide no benefit (except for the fact that it might get them paid). But what kind of memorial of the project plan and process would there be when the client needs to go back to this documentation for reference, troubleshooting, or validation? If the documentation is just a pile of pages in a binder, this deliverable provides no ongoing value.

However, a complete documentation package, whether hard copy or electronic (should be both), should provide the client with all the forensic evidence to negate the need to call back the PM, because the documentation would provide it at a glance. In fact, the review of this documentation before acceptance of project completion may provide the necessary punch list of outstanding deliverable items to mitigate a missing project deliverable or capability. Maybe the cabling contractor included the wiring diagrams but not the test results. Or maybe the integrator provided the equipment lists but not the configuration files. There are many reasons both before and after delivery that reliance on this final documentation can serve to protect both the client and all the resources, including the PM.

Let's say, for instance, after a Wi-Fi upgrade project, there are intermittent network issues in one building. The owner would want to look at the test results (that should have been) required before accepting the project as complete. The structured cabling performance tests, as well as the heat maps and software configuration used for the wireless control managers, should be readily available for the engineers to reference and double-check. Without this discrete data, assembled in a logical organization with detailed narratives and table of contents, the engineers may be looking for a needle in a haystack, or bypassing the documentation and calling the PM at home in a panic (then the integrator and then the cabling contractor). Which would be preferred?

PM Perspective

As a consultant, planner, and PM, I often joke that we sell our consulting services by the pound (of paper) and that we specialize in writing reports that no one ever reads. My favorite of all time is to ask the question, "Are we writing this report for someone to read, or are we making a club to hit someone over the head?" Although these comments may cast a cynical light on the need for documentation, this is a statement of wit within the truth. The reality is very few people will read that report, or review the entire project documentation, BUT when they do, it needs to be complete and accurate.

There is nothing more powerful than sitting in a status meeting with "the binder" and being able to field any question or answer any objection with a flip of a page to the right chapter and supporting documentation. In essence, the documentation is the proof in the PM's pudding.

KEY CONCEPTS

Before jumping headlong into the MAPIT® project planning process, there are a few more concepts that are salient to the role and process of project planning. Keep in mind once again, project planning is tactical—it is a component of an overall strategic plan. The PM may have been part of the strategic planning process, but if he or she wasn't, that has no bearing on the project. The PM must be focused like a laser on key milestones: project initiation, plan development, project execution, and project completion.

Project management is planning and management—planning about planning, planning about doing, planning about testing, planning about completion, and then executing the plan.

Project Planning

Project planning is the second part of any project after contracts and kick-off (project initiation). The PM must bring as many of the stakeholders into the initial kick-off meeting to set the expectation about the project scope, scale, and timeline. Key budgetary stakeholders may require additional meetings along the way to insure proper funding and availability of funds. Once all these initial activities have taken place, it is time for the PM to start development of the project plan.

Chapter 2—"Core Processes"—will provide a deep dive into the project planning process. Unlike strategic planning that you may have experienced in reading the book *FAIL TO PLAN, PLAN TO FAIL*, project planning requires a much higher, but not absolute, level of specificity. Whereas in strategic planning, we seek to define initiatives and projects in general terms, often taking efforts to define with general, all encompassing, details, project planning seeks to define as much as possible in the plan development phase. And for what can't be specifically defined, we make assumptions, and for the worst case scenario, we have the concept of progressive elaboration.

Assumptions

In chapter 2—Core Processes we will discuss in detail how to make and state assumptions. As the saying goes, "Don't assume, you will make an a** out of you and me." But a good project planner makes his or her living off assumptions. In fact, project planning is almost all about making assumptions. To develop a project plan, the PM must assume that the sun will rise tomorrow and the organization will still be there. He must also assume that what is working now will work tomorrow and that the resources currently in place will be available when they are needed.

Some assumptions are obviously safer than others. Whereas the sun will definitely rise tomorrow, it is not safe to assume that a particular resource will be available when the time comes. And if not, then he or she must engage, schedule, and confirm. It is from these assumptions that the PM refines and elaborates the task list.

Ultimately, the assumptions are also a shield the PM utilizes to protect himself or herself and his or her plan. By stating the assumptions at the onset of the planning, and progressively through the planning process, the PM provides the opportunity for the client, stakeholders, and resources to add their details, issues, and concerns. This is the opportunity to engage subject matter experts (SMEs) to enhance the accuracy and credibility of the planning process. Nothing is better than stating assumptions early in the planning process and having the assumptions tested and verified or rejected. The statement of assumptions is a challenge to the client and stakeholders to test their own understanding of their environment.

For instance, in a Wi-Fi implementation project, the PM might ask the IT director, "Can we assume all the cabling is at least Category 5e?" The IT director may say, "I think so, yes," but it is the obligation of the PM to validate this. A wrong assumption in this case could be a multimillion-dollar mistake. Table 1.3—"Dangerous Assumptions"—provides a list of dangerous assumptions. The PM is advised to go ahead and ask these questions

Table 1.3 Dangerous Assumptions

Project	Assumption	Potential Impact
Wi-Fi installation	All cabling is Category 5e.	Non-Cat5e cable won't support 802.11ac Wi-Fi antennae at 1Gbs.
Network upgrade	The Main Distribution Frame (MDF) in each school doesn't need additional cooling.	MDF rooms are overheating and need HVAC upgrades.
VoIP upgrade	All cabling is Category 5e.	Intermittent problems on phones and requirements to add new Cat5e cabling after the project.
LMS deployment	LMS is compatible with all platforms.	Compatibility problems for some students and some platforms impacting school-wide acceptance.
Classroom technology	All teachers have a desk for laptop and document camera.	1. May need to buy new desks 2. No room for new desks

in order to get some of these broad considerations on the table early in the planning process.

After reviewing this table, it's not hard to see that one dangerous assumption could be very costly. The network upgrade scenario that causes MDF rooms to heat up is in full cycle. This happened in schools all over the nation in the first round of network installations through the 1980s and 1990s. Core network switches and UPS systems were installed in MDF rooms designed with minimal or no cooling. Servers soon followed. As these rooms heated up, principals and IT directors opened doors, added fans, and some spent millions in air-conditioning (HVAC) upgrades and installations. In one case a large school district in Southern California used the cost benefit of collapsing all servers to a central data center, instead of installing air-conditioning in over 180 schools, to justify a $20 million data center. Now this trend is happening again as schools implement video security systems and install network video recorders (NVRs)—which are just servers—in MDFs. Here we go again with the fans.

Progressive Elaboration

Although the flowchart in figure 1.3—"Progressive Elaboration"—is for levity, it makes light of the concept of progressive elaboration. This project management concept holds that some tasks and activities may not be fully defined in the project plan. The PM uses a placeholder to represent a time-lapse and resource requirement that allows the planning process to continue.

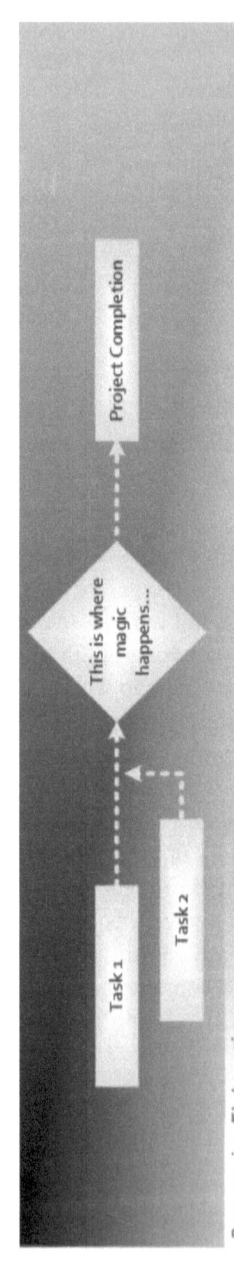

Progressive Elaboration

Figure 1.3 Progressive Elaboration

Then, as the preceding tasks are accomplished, and details of the project are finalized, the placeholder is replaced with real tasks, activities, and resources.

The inability of a PM to leverage this concept can paralyze a project. Think about the time a project was stalled because the PM was waiting to get an estimate, quote, or proposal back from a vendor or interdepartmental resource. The PM might report weekly, "We can't set a start date because so-and-so resource hasn't responded with the time and cost estimate." If this goes on beyond two weeks in a small- to medium-sized project, that PM should be fired!

PM Perspective

The quote in the previous paragraph is an example of throwing a project resource under the bus. In essence, if the PM were to make that statement, he or she would be placing blame upon that resource. A better way would be to state that additional assumptions and potential due dates are still being finalized for these resources.

The project planner or PM must engage with experts in each discipline in order to be able to create these placeholders. Every hardware and/or software deployment project WILL require a planning phase—is it two days, two weeks, or four months? The PM must have a sense from past experience how long this planning phase should last. Obviously, the more complex a project in scope and scale, the more planning will be required. The more subprojects, each subproject will require its own planning phase. The duration of each planning phase must be determined in order to build any realistic timeline for the project. The duration of the planning phase will also be affected by the planning resources and SMEs.

Progressive elaboration allows the project planner to skip over details that might bog down the planning process and impact implementation since nothing can really start without the project plan. Anything that is started is at risk of being incorrectly scoped, scaled, or specified. Therefore, progressive elaboration becomes a double-edged sword for the PM. If done without specific expertise, the whole program might be compromised. For instance, if the planner inserts a two-week planning phase at the beginning of the project but subsequently finds out that the expert is not available during that time frame, the whole project will be delayed. We'll go into this in detail in the project planning chapter.

Document Control

The PM must understand the concept of document control. Any document when in an incomplete, draft, or unedited format can become a noose by which to be hung. Project-related documents should be considered as the PM's property and guarded and protected as such. The PM must think of his or her documents as his or her tradecraft—arsenal. They can be used to memorialize project success, or they can be misused, by the PM and others to the detriment of the project. The PM should never allow multiple versions of plans, reports, timelines, or budgets to get out into the project world without discrete use and understanding of the purpose, scope, and intended distribution of the document.

Project documents are specific and purpose-driven—they are not operational support documents. That doesn't mean that they can't become part of an operation support document in the future, but for the purpose of the project, there must be a final deliverable document.

The PM cannot allow his or her work to be thought of as a living document and must manage all materials so they do not inadvertently become living documents, unless that is their intent. Some documents, like network configuration guides and software installation instructions, should be living documents for an IT department to provide access to the user base after project delivery and MUST be maintained by designated staff. But these are not project documents.

A project status report might be a living document, but for chronological purposes—not to give others the ability to change the historical archive of what actually happened. Herein lies the risk of the living document and why PMs must practice document control.

The PM must understand that most project documents *should not* be living documents. Meaning they are intended to be delivered in a completed state at a certain milestone. For instance, the project plan must be finalized and submitted before project execution can begin. Think of the confusion of preliminary project plans that get distributed with conflicting start dates or resources.

System documentation must be finalized and delivered as part of the project completion—neither of these should be living documents until the IT operations department makes them so and is obliged to maintain their accuracy as things change (this is part of Information Technology Infrastructure Library (ITIL) change management).

Document control is the concept that the PM must maintain a modicum of control over possibly premature or misleading documentation. For instance, if a PM creates a planning document and shares it (with edit permissions) electronically in a preliminary state, that PM loses control over the integrity and distribution of the document. He can't control if someone makes a change and/or sends it to someone else—in an incomplete or preliminary state.

There are several liabilities that may stem from lack of document control. First is electronic. The PM should always hesitate to share electronic versions of documents that are not final or collaborative works. In fact, the PM should use the "DRAFT" watermark feature on EVERYTHING! Sometimes it never comes off! Any electronic document shared in its native form (meaning a

.docx or .xlsx, as opposed to a .pdf) could be modified by someone else. The PM should protect all documents from modification and distribution. All reports, graphs, designs, and spreadsheets should be date and time stamped and clearly marked for its appropriate audience. All authorized viewers should be listed on the distribution list. Clear instructions should be made about who may view and keep these documents.

For weekly reports and status meetings, the PM should print hard copies and hand them out to attendees. All extra copies should be gathered and destroyed. For example, an early stage budget estimate might be lacking major components and communicate the wrong message in the early stages of a meeting. Having "DRAFT—DO NOT DISTRIBUTE" in the footer or header of every page can help in document control.

If meeting attendees ask for electronic copies, the PM should have a prepared speech about document control and authorized viewership and deliver a qualified "NO." Then of course, depending on the project influence of the individual, the PM must relent. If it's the client, then the PM should follow direction declaring the necessary caveats.

Project status reports should have an aging. Meaning that older status updates should be kept but moved down or grayed out in order to preserve the history of the updates. This can be a double-edged sword for the PM, but it will definitely shine the light on project status.

PM Perspective

Imagine one of your early planning documents with unqualified assumptions was suddenly distributed to project outsiders or district leadership. A firestorm of protests and objections might arise because of an early assumption or incorrect inference, or even a mistaken job title or misspelled name. You don't want to misspell the name or title of a cabinet member and have it distributed to other parties or even other districts. That PM will learn about document control in the most fearful way. Printing of these preliminary documents is also dangerous. Someone might find a discarded copy and think it's final.

Distribute hard-copy documents for project team members to mark up and hand back to you, so no lingering copies exist. If they need a copy, they can have it, with the markups, so the document is clearly not a final.

FIRST THINGS FIRST: PROJECT INITIATION

The first things that must happen before beginning any project plan are contracts, approvals, directives, or edicts. District staff don't just go around and think to themselves, "I think I'll do a Network Upgrade project for my organization" or "I'm going to buy 3,000 Chromebooks." Projects come from somewhere, typically a strategic plan or a new academic or administrative initiative. This strategic plan may not be a formal plan, but if it isn't, there is still some overall strategy that is calling for this project to occur. And for our purposes, it is for a school. And schools don't spend money without some instructional basis and authority. For example, a curriculum project that requires device mobility and one-to-one student devices will give rise to a Wi-Fi project and a device procurement project. Whether these are identified as two separate projects or one project does not matter. Figure 1.4—"Project Initiation"—details the typical tasks that occur in Project Initiation.

Sanction

Since these are formalities of initiation, they do not appear in the common workflow depictions of project planning. But of course, the first thing that must happen for any project is a sanction or directive. Projects are undertaken as part of a strategy, an edict from the top with permission and authorization to dedicate time and resources to an endeavor.

Next there must be a request or solicitation for proposals (RFP, informal or formal), contract award, and approval to move forward with the project. In fact, not only must there be resources to implement and execute the project, but there must be a resource to plan and manage the project. This sanction may be as informal as being told by the superintendent, "Yes, let's go ahead with the one-to-one project," but any PM would be encouraged to seek a formal directive to move forward with any major project or expenditure.

The PM would also be wise to obtain a formal request, directive, or edict. A PM might ask, "I will certainly begin working on the one-to-one project. Would you kindly send me an email directing me to begin this project?"

Project Name

Every project has a name. Or better stated, every project should have a name. Within the MAPIT® realm, every project *must* have a name. Without a name, the project cannot take on an identity and characteristic branding of its own. By having a name, the PM can become responsible for the project and can engage resources and stakeholders on behalf of the project. Without a name, the project cannot be owned and delivered successfully. That is not to say a software can't be selected and implemented without a project name, but no matter, it will have a name, even if it's just "Software Upgrade Project."

The name should allude to the instructional objective of the project or initiative. That's why one-to-one is not a good project name; although it is probably used in about every district, it's widely used not because of its academic

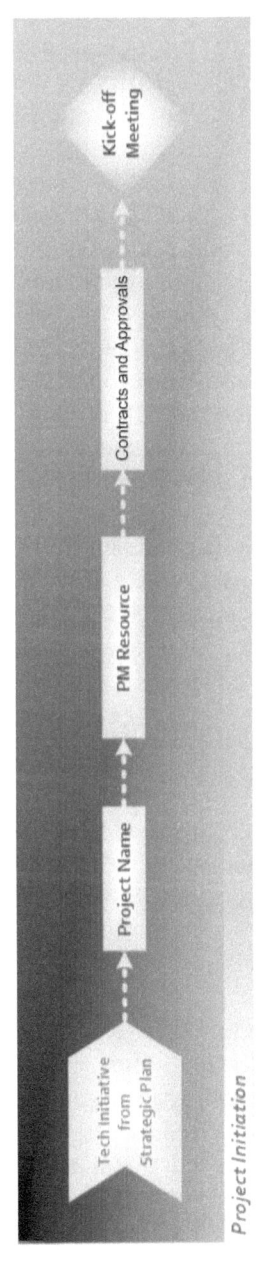

Project Initiation

Figure 1.4 Project Initiation

goals but because of its trendiness. "One-to-one" is inherently technology oriented and doesn't provide any insight or context for the project except that there are devices for each student. But should the district really be buying devices for students who already have multiple devices—probably better than the device the school is providing?—(sorry for the editorial .dv).

Just as branding is a major factor in marketing and sales, so is branding of the project name. What sounds more exciting, "Network Upgrade Project" or "Writing to Learn Project"? How about "Wi-Fi Project" versus "Mobile Learning Model"? All this discussion about the name of a project may seem silly, but the reality is, if you can't name your project, is there really a project? In fact, not naming a project is a way to diminish the importance of the project or endeavor. Let's say an individual school wants to implement a learning management system (LMS). What typically occurs is the LMS vendor will attempt to license the software to the entire school district in order to maximize discounting. This is not a bad thing. The school district would be wise to consider this and should initiate a study of LMS. This study is a project. It would logically be called the LMS selection project. But we're offtrack.

Once the software has been selected and licensed, the rollout and implementation of the LMS is the main project. It would require project planning, connectivity, computing resources, licensing, software implementation, and of course, training—training for the teachers, as well as the LMS administrators, and then ultimately the students. It would be called the "LMS NAME Implementation Project."

PM Perspective

When choosing a name for a project, it is always best to find a relevant, descriptive, and noble name that people will understand and want to support. What sounds better, Network Upgrade Project or Titan STEAM?

Project Management Resource

So it follows that every project must have a PM. That PM may not have the designation of project manager, but someone has to "make the project happen." It also follows that if the project management resource is not designated as such, then he or she will likely be held responsible for project success like a PM, but lacking authority or sanction as a project manager, and worse yet, likely also still responsible for his or her regular day-to-day responsibilities, which, in turn, affects the critical success factors tied to having a designated PM. This double duty, which is common in resource-constrained educational institutions, usually results in negative impacts in performance of both the project and the operational duties. This oft-repeated "lesson learned" still doesn't seem to gain common acknowledgment. When the IT director says, "When am I supposed to do this project, in my spare time?" The superintendent typically responds, "Wait a minute, that's your job."

Actually, the IT director's job is to convince the superintendent that he or she needs additional resources to manage that project—either someone else to help support your operational responsibilities or a project management resource to focus like a laser on just this project. Good luck!

Contracts and Approvals

If the school is looking for an outside resource for the PM, then contracts become an important project initiation component. The school must identify their consultant/PM, get a proposal or quote for services (which could easily require a formal bid process), and get these contracts through board approvals and final signatures BEFORE the PM will begin any activities—this can take weeks or even months with some school districts. Meanwhile, the clock will be ticking on the project, and the superintendent will be asking himself or herself why can't the IT director do this. Isn't that his or her job? Reminder, NO IT ISN'T.

This often becomes a point of philosophical efficiency of the assistant superintendent of business and the purchasing department. If they understand the concept of working with consultants, such as a dedicated PM resource, this can be a pretty streamlined process, but if they haven't come out of the dark ages and still don't understand why they need to go outside their organization and pay for these services, then someone needs to turn on the light!

In order to initiate a project between a consultant PM and a school, the following items should be agreed upon and communicated between all parties. Typically, before the PM can start, there must be the following documents and processes, signatures, all signed and original documents, contracts, proposals, addenda, as well as related agency contracts, and subcontracts, to the consultant company and the school district's purchasing department.

Contract

In order to begin any consulting engagement, project or outsourcing agreement, an agreement between the school and the PM should include the following items:

- Detailed scope of work
- Resource staffing schedule

- Project work plan
- Estimated labor cost
- Contract terms and conditions

Other contract specifics, such as deliverables, fixed-cost estimates, overtime rates, and assumptions should also be detailed in the contract. Absent a contract, a school may use a consulting agreement in order to procure PM services. This might be in the form of time-and-materials engagement using a purchase order (PO).

Oftentimes, this can be the silver bullet to getting things started. Using a PO for consulting services can allow a facilities, business, or IT department to engage with consultants in an "under the bid limit" month-to-month services contract. If necessary, this engagement can be used as a bridge to get project planning initiated while formal consulting agreements are solicited, awarded, and executed.

Time Tracking

Depending on the engagement, time tracking may be the billing control. This is not always the case, but it is likely the best way to monitor cost versus progress. For instance, if the project is not half over, but the PM has billed more than half his or her estimated time, the client stakeholder must ask the question if the contract estimated hours will be exceeded. And if so, what's the implication? Does the PM simply run out of hours, or is he or she bound to complete the scope of work regardless of the remaining hours? This is something the school program manager should be monitoring at the very least, a monthly basis, but more likely, a weekly basis, based on weekly reports.

Based on the contract type, timesheets should be used to invoice the client school as well as track any time payable to agencies or subcontracts. The school client must appoint and communicate to all stakeholders who will be authorized to represent them for timesheet signatures.

Invoicing

During the kick-off meeting, the client must be informed of the consultant PM's invoicing process. This may have to be supported and administered through the client's purchasing or accounts payable department. Invoicing procedures may be modified for the client's requirements, but monthly and twice-monthly is typical. More discussion of time tracking and invoicing will be discussed in chapter 3—Support Processes.

The Kick-Off Meeting

The kick-off meeting signifies the official beginning of the project to the rest of the world. Since this is at the project level as opposed to a strategic plan, the attendees of the project kick-off should only include the client, key stakeholders, and key internal resources. External resources might also be included, but that would assume they are either attending as an unbillable resource, or that they are already under contract and can bill the client directly for attending the meeting.

The act of scheduling of the kick-off meeting typically means that all the contracts and approvals described previously are complete, or at least are expected to be complete by the time of the meeting, which typically means that it's at the very least one-week out, probably more like two weeks for any medium to large project. One can see how one task or activity, such as scheduling a meeting, can impact the project significantly. What if all contracts and approvals are in hand, but the client is going on vacation for a week? Can we schedule the kick-off meeting while he or she's away? Better not.

Table 1.4—"Kick-off Meeting Agenda Template"—provides a template for almost any project kick-off meeting.

Logistics

The following is a checklist for items that should be discussed and established during the kick-off meeting and/or project initiation. Following are several

Table 1.4 Kick-Off Meeting Agenda Template

Agenda Item	Description
Introductions	Project manager, Client, Stakeholders, Resources
Schedule of planning process	Know hard dates and estimated milestones
Review of deliverables	Project objectives
	Operational systems—Commissioning
	Systems documentation
	Knowledge transfer and training
Discovery process	Schedule of departmental interviews
	Requests for documents and data
	Due dates for these items
Communications plan including:	Communications distribution list and key contact information
	Weekly or standing status meetings
	Reports and frequency
Logistics	Checklist provided

logistics questions that will lay the groundwork for how much access and how visible the project manager and resources will be:

- Where will we work?
- Can we work remotely?
- Where is the lab? Is it isolated from the production network?
- Do we have network connectivity?
- Do we have Internet connectivity?
- Will we have computers to access for administration?
- Are there security badges or other special access controls to the work area?
- Where should we park our cars?
- What is the attire?

Chapter 2

Core Processes: Creating the Project Plan

Figure 2.1—"Core Planning Processes"—details the plan development process. Notice that some of these subplans are developed simultaneously while others are sequentially dependent. In the end, there should be a very detailed implementation plan, timeline, resource plan, and project budget. Even though there may be a lot of subplans to research and develop, the PM must be very astute about his or her ability to develop this plan within a given time frame.

There is a time and duration for the planning of a project that must end with the finalized project plan that, once approved, triggers the project execution phase. This is not absolute, however. It may be possible to start certain parts of a project before the plan is finalized. For instance, in a 10Gbps core network upgrade, it may be understood that all new fiber optic backbone cabling will be required. Thus, the fiber optic backbone subproject may be initiated before the equipment list and configurations are finalized.

The important point is that at the beginning of any project is a planning process. This may be anywhere from 2 to 60 days based on the size and complexity of the project. But it shouldn't be just one day because it assuredly needs some research, design, consensus, resource planning, and documentation. It is *always* faulty to start a project and assume the plan that already exists is detailed enough to actually execute as a project. If a Gantt chart is created, the start date should include the plan development process, a milestone event that triggers execution, which leads right into site preparation, procurement, acquisition, provisioning, and implementation. The creation of this Gantt chart will be discussed in detail in this chapter.

Figure 2.2—"Core Processes"—details the explosion of each of the phases of the project planning process.

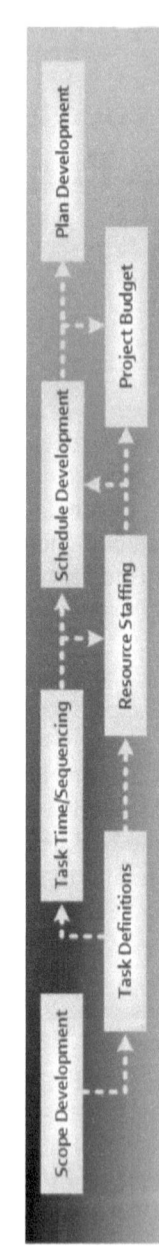

Core Planning Processes

Figure 2.1 Core Planning Processes

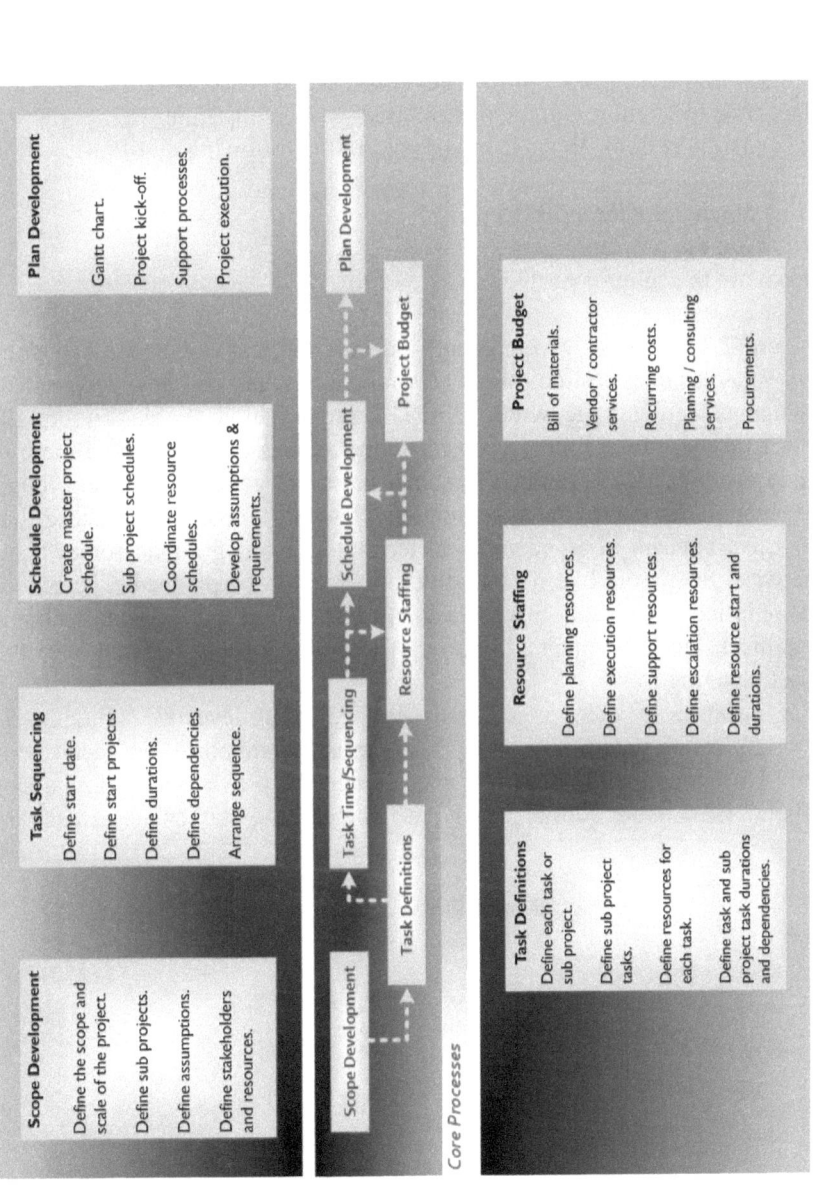

Figure 2.2 Core Processes

SCOPE DEVELOPMENT

Scope is one of the triple constraints along with time and budget. It is also the constraint that the PM has the most ability to control and manage. That is not to say that a successful project never has scope creep, only that time and budget tend to be more rigid and structured—especially time.

It is easiest to think about scope by asking the following questions:

- How much, how far, how deep?
- What are the projects?
- What are the subprojects?

Figure 2.3—"Scope Development"—details the tasks of Scope Development. Whereas the questions about how much, how far, and how deep reflect on scope as well as scale, within MAPIT® scope includes scale. First of all, the fact that you're defining a project scope alludes to the fact that there is already a project scope defined in somewhat more general terms and rough order magnitude (ROM) cost estimation. It would make logical sense that the project appears in an educational technology strategic plan somewhere. Otherwise there would be no initiative or project to be planned. The school leadership may know that there is a Wi-Fi installation or classroom technology project, but how much and how far become glaringly relevant once the project planning starts.

For instance, if there is a Wi-Fi project, what level of saturation is required? Better stated, how many users must be supported in each classroom? How much bandwidth will each student be provisioned? How about teachers? How about administrators and nonteaching staff? One can see by

Scope Development

Define the scope and scale of the project.

Define sub projects.

Define assumptions.

Define stakeholders and resources.

Figure 2.3 Scope Development

these sample questions that scope and scale could easily double or triple a project size (scale), cost, and deployment timeline. Yet each one of these questions, and more, will likely require specific answers in order to get to the actual scope and scale. Just recommending a Wi-Fi bandwidth provision of 10Mbps as opposed to 5Mbps for each student would have a massive effect on cost—likely almost double. But what is the basis for this provision?

In a classroom technology deployment project, the inclusion of one technology component in every classroom could have a huge impact on project cost. For instance, calculate the cost differential of installing interactive projectors in each classroom. For example, assume a $5,000 budget to install projectors and teacher laptops for each classroom in a school district with 1,000 classrooms. Then as an exercise, what if we added a document camera or even a number of student tablets to each?

Every additional component cost plus installation would be multiplied by 1,000. So, scope must be defined with as much specificity as possible. As far as scale is concerned, this is another area of defined constraint. If the general scope definition is all classrooms, does that also mean the band room, PE facilities, and special education classrooms? What about kindergarten and preschool classrooms? What about the classroom to be used by the Boys & Girls Club or after-school programs? Do elementary students have the same technology requirements as secondary school students? Do humanities classrooms require the same technology suite as the science classroom? What about ceramics? And then, why wouldn't we have some similar technologies in noninstructional areas such as libraries, conference rooms, and the multipurpose rooms?

It should be noted that the strategic planning process and ROM cost model should already have been developed to estimate the rough scale and cost of the project. But if not, it is time to get these details ironed out. At the tactical, or project level, the PM seeks to define the scope and scale in specific and all-encompassing terms. Once again, as in the strategic planning methodology, the bigger the scope, the bigger the budget must be, so the process of defining scope at this level is mission-critical.

There is a nicely granular approach to defining scope. Let's look as some examples.

Define Project Scope and Scale

The PM must learn to use subjective descriptions (as opposed to numerical and seemingly arbitrary language) in order to define scope and scale. Using language like "all classrooms" or "elementary classrooms" prefaced by "including" or "not including" provides very objective descriptions of scope without numbers or technical details. Table 2.1—"Project Scope and Scale"—provides examples of using general terms instead of seeming arbitrary numbers to define scope and scale.

Table 2.1 Project Scope and Scale

Project	Description	Scope/Scale
Wi-Fi installation	Installation of wireless management system, security, and antennas	All district locations including: • All classrooms • Administrative offices • Noninstructional areas • Exterior areas • 4Mbps per student device
VoIP upgrade	Implement VoIP telephony server(s) and IP phones.	Replace all phones, and place new phones as needed.
LMS deployment	License, host, deploy, and train LMS.	All teachers and students and instructional support staff
Classroom technology	Define, procure, deploy, and train classroom AV.	Every classroom

By using these more general types of descriptors for defining scope, the PM also communicates the logic—the "what and why"—of the scope. For instance, instead of saying 300 classrooms, which communicates a specific number without communicating that 300 comprises all classrooms, it is actually more descriptive to say "All Classrooms" or "All Secondary Classrooms." It would be fine to provide detailed numbers in the body of the report, but these details will likely need to be provided with a table or schedule.

Once the details of classroom technologies and configurations are explored, researched, and extrapolated in a project budget (more accurate than the ROM cost model), one will also be obliged to identify all the exceptions and special cases. For instance, when calculating the number of classrooms, the PM will need to know whether or not to include preschool classrooms, or classrooms used for special education or special clubs. What about classrooms that aren't currently being used, or conference rooms?

Special Ed classrooms often have different, more accessible technologies such as interactive input devices, large-format screens, and custom software applications. A sound reinforcement system that might be standard for "all" classrooms might be totally unnecessary in one of these classrooms. Science classrooms as well can easily be specified to require much more connectivity and specialized equipment. And if audio enhancement for the hearing impaired is required in some classrooms, should they be installed in all?

Scope and scale may also be inconsistent between school sites, not just between classroom types. In some districts, schools built before a certain date may have intercoms versus digital PBX systems. More commonly today, newer and modernized schools have Cat 6 cables and VoIP phones. How do these types of standards apply to the other schools? Do they warrant upgrades and associated funds more so than the newer, already modernized schools?

Really? Better ask the parents of the students in the newer schools. It could be wagered that they'd like to see the funds distributed evenly to all sites as opposed to more money for older sites.

Classroom technologies may well be the standard, or nonstandard, that a PM might perish over. Unless he or she is also the lead advocate for classroom technology for the district, it will be the obligation of the PM to take all input from all stakeholders and vet the final classroom configuration through all committees, leadership, and board members before any monies are spent.

Pity the IT manager who decided that iPads are going to be the standard for entirely technical reasons. The PM is empowered to seek the final solution from the deciders through development of an instructionally based use model, a significant level of consensus gathering, and to not be perceived as the sole decision maker. In fact, it would be best if the PM is seen as totally objective, and unbiased toward any technical solution, and seeking the best investment for the life cycle of the project.

The PM might have an ace-in-hole if he or she knows who are his or her primary advocates. When consensus is unreachable through more diplomatic means, such as the technology advisory committee, or cabinet workgroup, then it's time to pull out the trump card. If the PM's client has the authority, or if he or she can gain the advocacy of the cabinet or board member who does, then they can just implement it by edict. I sometimes ask my clients, do we want to take a vote or just shove it down their throats? Sometimes the latter is easier and cheaper!

Other ways to define scope would be to define "suites" or categories of implementation projects such as "all secondary science classrooms," "all kindergarten classrooms," or "noninstructional areas" to cover administration buildings, counseling offices, multipurpose rooms, gymnasiums, and stadiums. Wi-Fi coverage should also include saturation levels or performance capacity for a number of users.

Defining scope by user type or user class can also provide more "what and why" detail. For instance, "all teachers" or "all students" can easily define scope for user devices and "replace all phones" easily defines part of the scope and scale of a VoIP project. Defining scope and scale through the concept of suites can also provide a level of granular yet subjective description. An example would be science classrooms receive the "science technology suite" and the other classrooms get the "standard secondary suite."

Once again, using these types of subjective descriptors allows the communication of policy and logic. Arbitrary decision making always seems flawed by the nonbeneficiaries of any project or initiative. Nothing worse than walking into a classroom to admire your work progress and have a teacher say, "Why did that teacher get that, and I didn't?" Not so bad if you can explain why. Similarly, using the descriptor rather than an actual number also answers questions before they are asked. For instance, if the project is described as 300 classrooms, instead of as secondary classrooms, the nonbeneficiaries would ask, "How did you come up with 300 classrooms? Why can't you do 301 to include mine?" This is when I restrain myself from commenting, "It's not your classroom. It belongs to the school; you're just the current occupant." But I digress.

Define Subprojects

Almost every project is a series of subprojects. Table 2.2—"Subproject Definitions"—shows how subprojects might be defined in each of our scenarios. Each project has subprojects of different scope or scale. Note how the classroom technology subprojects are different in scope and scale.

Define Assumptions

Although it would seem assumptions would be defined before scope and scale, it is actually easier to do it afterward. After each project or subproject scope and scale definition, the PM can ask himself or herself, "What assumptions am I making?" This mental exercise will help the PM to insure that he or she is not making logical leaps or broad generalizations. For instance, in a VoIP

Table 2.2 Subproject Definitions

Project	Subprojects	Scope/Scale
Wi-Fi installation	New Cat 6 cabling to support WAPs	All district locations including: • All classrooms
	New wireless control system	District-wide cloud-based solution
	WAP installations	All district locations including: • All classrooms
VoIP upgrade	Install new Cat 6 cables	All existing phone locations
	Implement IP PBX, VoiceMail, e911	District-wide implementation
	Deploy new IP phones	All existing phone locations
LMS deployment	License and deploy hosted LMS	Secondary teachers and students
	Training for teachers	Secondary teachers
	Training for students	Secondary students
Classroom technology	Classroom AV	Every elementary classroom
	Classroom AV and student devices	Every middle school classroom
	Classroom AV and student devices	Every high school classroom

upgrade, existing cabling is almost always called into question. Deciding to install all new cabling versus using older existing cabling could be the difference between project success and failure. While deciding not to upgrade the cabling at the risk of having poor performance or intermittent problems, the cost of new cabling could easily double or triple the cost estimate and kill the project entirely.

Another common mistake in the LMS scenario might be software or hardware compatibility. Does the new LMS support older versions of a browser that is being used in all the current computer labs? Does the LMS require special keyboard characters that aren't available on some tablets? What about standardized tests and their hardware requirements? The exercise of describing the assumptions should help uncover some of these hidden project risks. Some of these assumptions, once tested and validated, may cause changes to the scope, scale, and overall project plan. It may even cause a delay or stoppage, but it likely means that a project failure may have been avoided or mitigated.

Table 2.3—"Project Assumptions"—details examples of assumptions tied to each project and subproject.

Table 2.3 Project Assumptions

Project	Description	Assumptions
Wi-Fi installation	Installation of wireless management system, security, and antennas	• All new Cat 6 cabling will be installed for each WAP. • Cloud-based control system will support all connections at full capacity.
VoIP upgrade	Implement VoIP telephony server(s) and IP phones	• All existing phones will be replaced with new IP phones. • No new phones will be added in this project. • All existing Cat 5e cable or higher may be used. • Cat 5 or lower cabling may be used at 100Mbps IP phones.
LMS deployment	License, host, deploy, and train LMS	• All teachers and students and instructional support staff • LMS is compatible with all existing devices and browsers.
Classroom technology	Define, procure, deploy, and train classroom AV	• Every classroom • Also to include conference rooms and library/media centers • No new power circuits will be required. • Five-year or older interactive whiteboards (IWBs) will be replaced.

Not all assumptions are clear cut on the outset of a project. For example, did the last bullet on the classroom technology scenario in table 2.3—"Project Assumptions"—catch your eye? This assumption should actually be a policy and scope definition as opposed to an assumption. But it is an example of what might happen in a classroom AV technology refresh. What to do with the old stuff? Is five years the true life cycle of the IWB? If so, then it truly begs a question of the wisdom of the overall investment, but the assumption itself also begs practical questions like:

- Does this mean that next year I have to go around and replace the next round of five-year-old IWBs?
- What is the additional labor cost of removing an IWB including patching and painting the walls?
- Is the patching and painting to be done by the installing contractor? This can be a complex question because of state trade and prevailing wage laws.

PM Perspective

Each assumption must be tested and validated by as many resources as possible. But the PM must advance to the next step in order to do this. During the plan development process, the PM must engage with the client and resources to validate assumptions. This can be done during the next weekly status meeting if the planning schedule includes more than one standing meeting.

If there is no standing meeting prescheduled to get the assumptions vetted, the PM must decide either to call a meeting (which may take a week to schedule) or solicit each client and resource individually or in groups to vet the assumptions in front of all the critical parties. Since these types of interactions may be verbal personal communications, the PM should follow up each interaction with a confirming e-mail that creates a memorial of the discussion and allows the resource/client to confirm electronically.

Define Stakeholders and Resources

Although the term "stakeholder" has already been used throughout this book, it should be clearly defined. Stakeholders are individuals directly impacted and reliant on the success of the project. The superintendent of the school district is always a stakeholder if he or she wants to be. This may also be true for any particular board member. Beyond that, the PM must understand the "stake" each individual and resource has in the project. Table 2.4—"Stakeholders"—provides an example of how to categorize and understand each stakeholder's influence and interest in the project.

Table 2.4 Stakeholders

Type	Examples	Influence	Interest	Process Management and Communication
End user	Students Teachers Administrators Staff	Low	Medium to high	Low to medium
Executive	Superintendent Board member Assistant superintendent over project	High	Medium to high	High
Resource	Project manager Vendor engineer Purchasing manager IT staff	Medium to high	High High Medium High	Medium High during involvement
Outlier	Parents Community members	Low Low	Medium to high Low to medium	Low to medium

Stakeholders can be defined in levels of influence, interest, or impact (impact on the project, or impacted by the project). High-influence stakeholders are members who have decision-making control over the project or are highly critical resources of the project, like the superintendent or the director. High-interest stakeholders may not be influential in project control or decision making but will be directly impacted by the project, like the teachers using wireless student devices.

Medium-influence stakeholders might be project administrators or impacted staff. Medium-interest stakeholders might be subproject resources or providers of products or services. The criticality of these medium influencers may spike during the project implementation and then wane away.

Low-influence stakeholders might be end users or indirect resources. Low-interest stakeholders are users or resources on the periphery or in supporting roles of the project.

Dealing with Detractors and Low-Influence Stakeholders

Oftentimes, these are users who may be losing influence they once held before the larger-scale initiative. That doesn't mean their input is no longer valuable or their objections shouldn't be voiced; it simply means that ultimately, that individual doesn't have that much formal or organizational authority and can't affect the course or decision-making processes of the project.

Think of the site media tech that formerly supported all the teachers at the site on a specific platform, such as iPads. If a Chromebook project managed by the district comes to the site, this person must either adapt to the new platform or be seen as an obstructionist. And although adoption is the obvious right direction for that person, sometimes this loss of influence can trigger self-destructive tendencies, especially if that resource is emotionally and technically invested in that platform. It is only mentioned here because it is such a common occurrence.

It is often this type of vocal but noninfluential stakeholder who may attempt to wield his or her influence (or lack of) and cause dissension or make waves in the project, and must be ignored or bypassed—of course, with tacit approval of the real high-influence stakeholders.

Many schools and school districts have this individual who although without budget or decision-making authority injects himself or herself into the planning process, courting as many supporters as possible so as to turn critical decision points into an all-out civil war. This person likely was an early adopter of a technology or platform, who was probably recognized early on as a pioneer of the use model and, because of this history and standing, had influence at the site or district level in the past, but has recently been disempowered by the large-scale implementation process. Meaning the PM is the evil implementer from the dark side, a threat to his or her sovereignty, the undoer of his or her master plan, the ever-vilified "consultant."

Think of the iPad versus Chromebook decision, or the Mac versus PC camps from the past. The PM must be systematic and unemotional in formalizing the research, cost modeling, and ultimate design decisions in order to delegitimize or invalidate the objections and dissension caused by these detractors. The PM must never be the primary advocate in these design decisions, merely the compiler of information and the documenter of consensus. The PM is best advised not to take sides in a political dogfight but must be Machiavellian in his or her actions and decisions. Doing what is in line with the defined project objectives is # 2, while doing what the client wants is still # 1. Hopefully, these two are aligned.

The PM responds and relates to the stakeholders with process management and communication. The higher the level of influence and interest, the more process and communication will be required to keep them informed and satisfied with the project.

Processes might be weekly status meetings where the PM provides an opportunity for the stakeholders to ask questions and interact with the project resources. Communication is always a combination of verbal, written, and formal communications. Anything verbal should also be followed with a written communication—e-mail is perfect. A communications plan—detailed in chapter 3—will detail the type, frequency, and distribution of each type of communication.

Stakeholders can also be categorized by the type of interaction or level of influence they have on the project. These four stakeholder types can be used to help the PM understand their need for and level of communication: end user, executive, resource, and outlier.

End User

These stakeholders will be the logical beneficiary of the project. For instance, in a Wi-Fi project, everyone within the school's Wi-Fi coverage becomes an end user of the system, students, teachers, administrators, staff, and even parents and police. Their influence on the project is low, but their interest is medium to high.

End users may require very little if any management or communication until the project is completed. Once they become reliant on the Wi-Fi, their interest in the support of the Wi-Fi will be high. But that's after the project is completed. If everything goes as planned, the end users can be the project's biggest advocate or detractor. Think of a school where everyone is on Wi-Fi and can use it effectively, or another school where the students say, "Wi-Fi sucks," and the teachers can't plan their lessons based on connectivity.

Executive

Project executives have governance and/or decision-making influence on a project. For instance, an assistant superintendent of business will have budgetary control of a project yet may have low interest. The superintendent will be the ultimate executive of the project if he or she has any interest. The superintendent may be totally disengaged from a VoIP project, but if the phones are not working, both influence and interest will go through the roof! These stakeholders require as much process management and communication as needed to keep them satisfied and should be the focus of the communications plan.

Resource

Project resources have direct influence and interest in a project but likely for a limited amount of time. The installing vendor of the Wi-Fi system is a key stakeholder but only until the project is successfully delivered. Then their influence and interest subside. However, the IT staff who inherit the support of the Wi-Fi system will move from low influence to high influence once the system is handed over.

Project resources will have a high level of influence and interest in the planning stages weeks before their necessary execution engagement. Their requirements for process management and communication will also peak and subside with their project involvement. The most important point that will be of specific focus in chapter 3—"Support Processes"—is the engagement of these resources, both in the planning and execution phases.

Outlier

Outliers are project stakeholders that must be addressed but in reality have little influence but medium to high interest like we referred to earlier. Another example of an outlier is the PTA member or newspaper reporter. They have no influence but an opinion and a pair of ears (or many ears) and have a personal interest. A good PM will know who, if any, of these outliers will require additional process management or communication in order for his or her project to remain under a good light. One critical outlier talking to a board member can sabotage the perceived success of a project.

The salient point about stakeholders is that anyone can be a stakeholder. They may be an outlier with no influence but high interest and may be in communication with an executive stakeholder. Alternately, an executive with high influence may have low interest, but that doesn't mean that he or she doesn't require a high level of management and communication. Leadership needs to have high-level but timely and accurate information, so keeping status high on the communication to high-influence stakeholders is good practice.

PM Perspective

The PM may learn through the duration of the project that the level of process management and communications may decrease or increase for a given stakeholder and that his or her awareness to these changing needs is paramount to a successful project delivery. For instance, if the superintendent has low interest in a VoIP project, but then his or her phone stops working, the PM better be ready to provide the history and processes leading up to the outage and raise this process management and communication to HIGH.

TASK DEFINITIONS

Tasks are actions—things that happen—things made to happen. The PM is the task master. Once again, asking the following questions:

- What are the tasks?
- What is the scope of each task?
- Who (what resources) will perform the task?
- How do we engage the resources?

Figure 2.4—"Task Definitions"—details the process of defining the project tasks and subprojects. The PM must learn that everything is a task. A report is a task. A conversation is (was) a task. A phone call is a task. Not every task must be fully documented, but the PM is well advised to err on the side of too much task documentation rather than the alternative. This task

Task Definitions

Define each task or sub project.

Define sub project tasks.

Define resources.

Define durations and dependencies.

Define milestones.

Figure 2.4 Task Definitions

documentation can always be used in the compiled systems documentation and final deliverable and might be invaluable when the time comes to justify or validate some discussion, meeting, conversation, or decision in the future.

Some activities are made up of multiple tasks but ultimately summarized as a single task. PMs can be haunted by the mystery tasks of a resource who completed a task but didn't formally report to the PM of its completion. By directly engaging with each resource about each task—before and after—is the only way for the PM to stay apprised of all tasks and activities of a project. That may mean that the PM must communicate to vendor resources, subcontractors, and other third parties. It is never acceptable for the PM to point to project risk and then blame the resource. It may require several "bird-dog" phone calls and e-mails to make sure that something is on track and on time.

The PM should become familiar with using some sort of project management tool to help identify, organize, reorganize, and plan tasks and activities. Using a tool like Microsoft Project is probably the easiest way to rapidly prototype and develop a working project plan; however, there are also many task-based web applications that are better at managing day-to-day tasks at a more granular level than a Gantt chart.

PM Perspective

It should be noted that a Gantt chart is never the complete plan. The Gantt chart is simply a graphic representation of the identified tasks and activities and their dependencies—it has no connection to reality unless each task is specifically acted upon by the resource. The Gantt chart is usually most effectual in the justification and initial communication of the plan.

The Gantt may lose its relevance completely or merely become part of the project deliverable documentation as the project moves to execution and completion. Once the project is complete, it's as if the Gantt chart never existed. No one ever goes back to a Gantt chart unless to argue about deliverable dates or develop chronologies for liquidated damage lawsuits.

The PM should also be warned that the Gantt chart is for planning, not necessarily for execution. Execution is a completely different practice. Although risks and changes may cause changes to the plan, these changes must be planned, assimilated, and absorbed into the execution process.

The more complete the plan, the better the execution, but the Gantt chart depicting the plan doesn't provide the same support for tracking the project during execution, unless the tracking Gantt chart function is utilized by the PM to do just that. Oftentimes, there are so many additional tasks and communications that are used to track, monitor, and report execution that the maintenance of the tracking Gantt falls by the wayside to more effectual communications such as status reports and actual versus projected budget expenditures.

As the PM starts to identify tasks, activities, resources and dependencies, the flexibility of the project planning tool rises to the highest-level of importance. Think of the old index card methodology, where the PM might write a task on each index card, add details about resources and durations, and then physically lay them out in sequence by dependencies. MS Project has the flexibility to allow the PM to do these types of manipulations and "what if" exercises to support 90% of medium-sized projects. Of course, larger projects, like building a school, should be left to the larger project management database systems to be managed and maintained by schedulers, construction managers, and program managers.

Short of using MS Project, many other tools can work, including:

- Word or Google Docs—Using tables in MS Word or Google Docs can be a good tool to define, describe, and organize tasks and activities. These tables lack the Gantt charting capability but can easily be set up like a calendar or timeline. It also doesn't allow for multiple simultaneous tasks and interdependencies because the table rows and columns become too complex to manage and manipulate, but tables do allow for more detailed descriptions because of the text-based cells, which in execution may be more significant to reporting status and risks than the graphical representation of tasks.
- Excel or Google Sheets—Using a spreadsheet for task and activities allows a PM to utilize the cells, dates, and color features to help organize tasks and activities. Once again, spreadsheets don't typically output a Gantt chart but can be very effective for managing many tasks, resources, and dates at a higher detail level than MS Project.

Schedules and timelines can easily be created and manipulated in a spreadsheet, but the cells are more limited for detailed textual entries than tables, and the dependencies must be managed manually or through database functions. Another advantage of using a spreadsheet for tracking tasks and activities is the ability to calculate dates, durations, and resource hours.

However, as helpful and important these calculations can be, the smallest error or fat-finger typo can undo all the benefits provided by the spreadsheet. Remember that anytime a spreadsheet is utilized in project management or cost modeling, intensive quality assurance of spreadsheet practices and data integrity must be implemented. Recall the time a simple copy/paste or the auto-undo reflex caused you to question how many times this operation might have compromised the accuracy or validity of the data in your plan.

- Visio or Google Drawing—These types of drawing tools including MS PowerPoint provide tools for creating Gantt charts, but these types of charts are mostly utilized in the early concept phase or formal presentation of the project to make visually attractive Gantt charts. Once into a real project, these drawing tools may require more work than the benefit provided to the PM and project.

Define Each Task or Subproject

Ultimately the PM will utilize several tools and methods to plan and manage tasks and activities, not the least of which is e-mail. Electronic mail becomes the document(s) of record because the fact that e-mail is ubiquitous (everyone has one), it is documentation (requires authorship) and is date and time stamped. So while e-mail will likely become the tool for memorializing and communicating, other tools such as report formats, project timelines, and bills of materials will also come into play in memorializing tasks and activities.

MS Word or Google Docs can be effectively used for all formal communications in the form of plan and report templates. Once the tool is determined, the process of task definition is a two-step process: (1) name the task and (2) describe the task. Sometimes the task is really a subproject; for instance, in the Wi-Fi project, installing all the structured cabling to support the new wireless access points would likely be a project in and of itself, with a scope and vendor contract, within the Wi-Fi project. In fact, any multischool structured cabling project would likely require a request for proposal (RFP), which is a complex process requiring formal bidding, performance and technical specifications, and board approvals.

The PM must be cognizant of the granular level of detail for each project, subproject, or task. Once again the flexibility of the planning tool becomes key. A tool that allows multiple levels of granularity, plus the ability to expand or collapse project tasks, is great for these purposes but is less conducive to managing projects with a large variety of resources needing detailed descriptions of tasks, resources, scope, and scale.

In these cases the Gantt chart becomes secondary to project management practices and procedures. Meaning that sometimes maintenance of the Gantt chart becomes a task in itself, and the PM must determine if the ongoing need to update the Gantt chart is adding value to the project. For instance, having a Gantt chart for laying out site schedules might actually be adding constraints or interdependencies where they don't exist.

If the Wi-Fi project is over multiple sites laid out in sequence in a Gantt chart, it may not in reality reflect other implementation factors that affect the vendor. Maybe the types of Wireless Access Points (WAP) required for an installation are not available; therefore, the vendor may reorganize the schedule of sites. Or the sites are undergoing construction and won't be available until later in the original deployment plan. The PM cannot let his or her investment in planning take priority or precedence over practical constraints.

Table 2.5—"Task Definitions"—provides an example of task names and scope and scale. This exercise identifies each task and activity. It's clear to

Table 2.5 Tasks Definitions

Project	Tasks and Activities	Scope/Scale
Wi-Fi installation	1. Structured cabling 2. Wi-Fi control system installation 3. WAP installation 4. Testing and verification	1. District-wide guidelines 2. Licensing and hosting 3. Vendor scope 4. Vendor scope
VoIP upgrade	1. Structured cabling 2. IP PBX host 3. Dial plan 4. VoiceMail 5. Auto attendant 6. Redundancy 7. E911 8. Testing and verification	1. All new phone locations 2. Licensing and hosting 3. District-wide 4. All users 5. All sites 6. All sites 7. District-wide 8. Vendor scope
LMS deployment	1. Licensing and hosting 2. Teacher professional development 3. Student training	1. All secondary teachers and students 2. Secondary teachers 3. Secondary students
Classroom technology	• Interactive AV • Sound reinforcement • Teacher devices • Student devices	1. Primary classrooms 2. Secondary classrooms 3. Other instructional areas

see that each task could be a long list of subtasks, when detailed to the Nth level. As mentioned earlier, the structured cabling requirement in both the Wi-Fi and the VoIP scenarios would likely be subprojects requiring site surveys and a formal bid process if on a district-wide scale.

Once task definitions start moving into the more granular details of the project planning and execution planning, the PM may determine that the Gantt chart is no longer the central project document and no longer provides significant project management value or benefit. That doesn't mean that it loses its value as a status reporting tool, but it is no longer necessarily supporting the day-to-day detail management of the project.

This can be determined by simply asking, "Who's looking at this chart besides me?" If the answer is no one, then the PM can examine if it's helping him or her in his or her process management efforts. If the answer is no, then the chart can go by the wayside. That doesn't mean it won't become important again later, so this decision to let the chart perish is certainly one to consider carefully.

Define Subproject Tasks

If a task is determined to be a subproject, then at some point the subproject tasks must also be defined, resourced, and scheduled. The concept of progressive elaboration comes up again here as the subproject may be large or small. It may impact the whole project or not at all. But the fact that the PM has included it in the project tasks means it holds some key relevancy or interdependency to the project. Once again, the planning tool that allows the PM to expand and collapse subprojects can be very helpful to the PM.

The PM must determine if the subproject requires its own PM and separate resources. Actually, there is no question if the subproject requires its own PM, just who that PM is. If it's the main project's PM (you), then the question must be asked: Do you have time and resources to support this subproject? If the answer is really, no, then the PM must adjust constraints in the plan, engage additional resources, or develop a risk assessment.

Define Task Resources

Project and task resources are the individuals and companies providing implementation (planning and execution) services to the project. Where the vendor might provide the equipment, the IT staff might be doing the installation. How the equipment is procured is different from how the IT staff are engaged. If the vendor is to do the installation, then the task of defining the installation standards and practices becomes a very important component of the quality assurance plan—one of the support processes to be discussed in chapter 3—Support Processes. The installation requirements or execution processes will become the specifications that bidders will use to develop their competitive estimates for their proposals, so identifying each resource for each task becomes an important point of investigation for the PM.

For instance, a common mistake made when developing specifications for network upgrades is the requirement of additional infrastructure and facilities. The IT director works with the PM to define the bandwidth, density, core, and edge devices and puts the installation out to bid. But is there enough power and rack space for the equipment? The PM would be wise to recognize these infrastructure requirements and (1) include power requirements and installation practices for the power and rack space in the formal bid, (2) engage the district maintenance and operations staff to do the work ahead of the vendor, or (3) engage an electrical contractor to do the work ahead of the vendor.

All three of these scenarios will cost much more money than the cost of the equipment and installation alone. And number 2 may be completely out of the question at some school districts. So the lesson here is that the electrical contractor must be one of the resources identified early in the planning stages. This information will aid in determining the scope of each resource, which in turn will help determine their method of engagement.

For instance, engagement of the district Maintenance & Operations (M&O) department may simply require an M&O work order, but because of the scale and time constraint, the M&O department may determine that their in-house staff cannot perform this project. Which department will engage the electrical contractor? Will the PM put it out to bid, or might he or she rely on the M&O department's regular vendor of its individual cable upgrades?

In the LMS deployment scenario, the vendor may provide the execution, but the training may be provided by another company, or possibly an independent contractor. How will this training component be engaged? What about for the project planning process? Does the training contractor need to be engaged as an SME for the planning process? And for the student testing, who will deliver these modules? Teachers, volunteers—do they require pizza and soda?

Defining the task resources will help the PM determine how each of these resources will be engaged. Are they in-house resources? Contractors? Consultants? How will they be contracted? Purchase order? Bid or RFP? Table 2.6—"Task Resources Engagement"—provides sample resource descriptions for the four scenarios and how each resource might be engaged. Each state has guidelines for public contracting that might directly affect

Table 2.6 Task Resources Engagement

Project	Tasks	Resource	Procurement Method
Wi-Fi installation	1. Structured cabling 2. Wi-Fi system installation 3. WAP installation 4. Testing and verification	1. Cabling contractor 2. Vendor 3. Vendor 4. Vendor	1. Formal bid 2. PO or RFP 3. PO or RFP 4. PO or RFP
VoIP upgrade	1. Structured cabling 2. IP PBX installation 3. Dial plan 4. VoiceMail 5. Auto attendant 6. Redundancy 7. E911 8. Testing and verification	1. Cabling contractor 2. Vendor 3. Vendor/IT 4. Vendor/IT 5. Vendor/IT 6. Vendor 7. Vendor 8. Vendor	1. Formal bid 2. PO or RFP 3. PO or RFP 4. PO or RFP 5. PO or RFP 6. PO or RFP 7. PO or RFP 8. PO or RFP
LMS deployment	1. Licensing and hosting 2. Teacher prof dev. 3. Student training	1. Vendor 2. Ed tech 3. Tech teachers	1. PO 2. Internal—District 3. Internal—Site
Classroom technology	• Interactive AV • Sound reinforcement • Teacher devices • Student devices	Vendor	Formal bid or RFP

how vendors, contractors, and consultants might be engaged. For instance, in California, a school district *shall* let any contracts in excess of $50,000 for equipment or services. Understanding these state and local codes will be critical to being an effective PM in any public agency.

Define Durations and Dependencies

Task durations are estimates based on know constraints, historical data, SMEs, or a trade contractor/consultant of how long a particular task may take. The PM is well advised to engage an SME or trade contractor/consultant to estimate durations for any task he or she is not intimately familiar with. For instance, if the PM has an IT background, he or she better work with an electrical contractor to properly estimate power upgrades required ahead of the network upgrade.

Just as important, the M&O versus outside contractor question may introduce additional lead time. Whereas a work order to M&O may affect work to be done in the following week, an RFP for electrical contractors may take eight weeks to procure, and then the actual execution duration following, if all goes well.

Similarly, the PM should get an LMS professional development duration estimates from the LMS training provider. It might be easy to build two weeks of training into a project plan, but are the training resources available? Are in-service hours and substitute teacher-hours available? Will the training be mandatory? Oftentimes, these closure tasks and activities may be the hardest to estimate as well as gain sign-off.

Define Milestones

Milestones are events that mark a significant point in the project—a plan completion, or subproject ending, or of course, the start of execution or the project closure. The milestone can be represented in the MS Project document with a duration of zero, and predecessors of all tasks and subprojects that must be completed before the milestone is achieved. The more predecessors to a milestone, the more tasks and activities are in the critical path of the milestone. Table 2.7—"Project Milestones"—shows the major milestones common to almost all education technology projects. A much more detailed project milestones table is discussed in chapter 3—Support Processes.

Table 2.7 Project Milestones

Milestone	Description
Project initiation	The tasks and activities required to formally initiate a project are used to set and plan the expected start date of the project. May be used to trigger the contract of engagement or the kick-off meeting.
Plan completion	Every project starts with a project planning phase; this milestone marks the end of planning, estimating, and justifying and marks the beginning of procurement, acquisition, and execution.
	Should there be a gap or elapsed time between plan completion and execution? If there are high-level approvals, such as board or budget, then there might need to be an estimated delay between the two. Or possibly, the execution must start on a given day, such as first day of summer break, and then the planning may be completed weeks before the execution milestone, which is fixed in time.
Phase completion	This might be the end of a major subproject that lies in the critical path of the main project, or the completion of a phase such as the planning or execution phase.
Project completion	This milestone should be triggered by actual testing, validating, commissioning, acceptance, and operational hand-off tasks such as knowledge transfer and training.

Core Processes: Creating the Project Plan 49

> **Task Sequencing**
>
> Define start date.
>
> Define start projects.
>
> Define durations.
>
> Define dependencies.
>
> Arrange sequence.

Figure 2.5 Task Sequencing

TASK SEQUENCING

As can be seen in the flowchart at the beginning of the chapter, figure 2.1—"Core Planning Processes," the process of developing task definitions provides inputs to two related processes of task sequencing and resource staffing. The PM will find that in the process preceding, Task Definitions, some of the time and sequencing details will be apparent. In this subprocess, the PM will define specific dates, durations, and dependencies to develop a logical and practical ordering of events. Asking these questions, the PM will begin to order the tasks according to scheduling constraints and dependencies:

- What are the initiation milestones of each task?
- What are the priorities of the tasks?
- What are the dependencies?
- What are the external timing factors?
- What are the timing constraints and expectations?

Figure 2.5—"Task Sequencing"—shows the steps to determining the sequence of the tasks and subprojects. Once again, the tool that provides the most flexibility to define tasks, durations, and dependencies is MS Project. The Gantt chart views can be directly manipulated and either hard dates or predecessors can be defined, altered, and reordered.

Define Start Date

The start date is a milestone. For most projects the start date should be before or on the date of the kick-off meeting. Assuming that contracts of services

50 Chapter 2

or dates of commitment of resources are real engagements, these milestones become the start of the project. There might be multiple start dates:

- Board or contract approval
- Notice to proceed
- Purchase order
- Kick-off meeting

Any of these may become the "official" start date. The most important factor is that the start date is some time after the project management resource is functionally and contractually engaged to start making things happen. No contracted PM or consultant will kick off a project without a means for getting paid.

Define Start Projects

The start project or initial projects are the tasks that will officially and technically initiate the project. Usually this is the kick-off meeting. Table 2.8—"Start Projects"—provides examples of these.

Table 2.8 Start Projects

Project	Tasks	Start Project(s)
Wi-Fi installation	• Structured cabling • Wi-Fi system installation • WAP installation • Testing and verification	• RFP development, solicitation, and award recommendation • Board approval/NTP • Installation and implementation
VoIP upgrade	• Structured cabling • IP PBX installation • Dial plan • VoiceMail • Auto attendant • Redundancy • E911 • Testing and verification	• RFP development, solicitation, and award recommendation • Board approval/NTP • Installation and implementation
LMS deployment	• Licensing and hosting • Teacher professional development • Student training	• Board approval—Purchase order • Implementation • Professional development and training
Classroom technology	• Interactive AV • Sound reinforcement • Teacher devices • Student devices	• RFP development, solicitation, and award recommendation • Board approval/NTP • Installation and implementation

Define Durations

Task durations are assigned in blocks by the PM and should be done liberally. In large complex projects, nothing happens in four hours. A school or district can't engage a contractor to come on-site to do large-scale work without a procurement cycle, be it a purchase order or an informal bid. The PM should assign task durations in the scale of full days, or full weeks, or even full months. Keeping in mind 5-day workweeks, one week is 5 days, two weeks is 10 days duration, and two months is eight weeks or 40 days duration.

The PM should think of time in unit blocks of elapsed time as opposed to time on task. If the engineer or SME says something should take three days, he or she is only thinking about his or her actual time on task. What about procurement, delivery, communications, downtime scheduling, facilities preparation, access to facilities, and whatever other factors that could take additional time? The project management tool should automatically not schedule work days on weekends and holidays.

These estimates and allocations will become the metrics and milestones for project success. Oftentimes, unrealistic time estimates can cause a project to go way over schedule, when in fact, if the time estimates were more realistic, the project would take the same amount of time but not be off schedule. Time is a constraint best manipulated in the project planning phase as opposed to the execution phase—by then it's too late and you're already off schedule.

There's a saying in project planning, "Take the engineer's estimate and double it, then triple it!" This is not always the case, but it's better to be ahead of a long schedule than late on a tight schedule. This also assumes that the planner has the luxury of no restrictive completion date. When projects are planned in reverse from a specified completion date, the duration estimates, and task sequencing will be the the key factors for fitting the project into the targeted completion date.

The PM must have a keen understanding of the reality behind due dates and completion milestones. The more time is constrained, the more tasks and activities must be executed simultaneously, or overlapping, and additional resources engaged as a contingency. Then the question must be asked: Does the PM have enough time to manage all these simultaneous projects?

It is different to want something done before school starts (hard target date) versus completion sometime this year (soft target date), but that doesn't mean that the PM should extend durations beyond reason. There are also very hard target dates, such as cutting over a data center over winter break. Not only must everything be ready to go on the start date, but all the work must be completed simultaneously and work together by the end of the break. As much preparation and preconfiguration must be done before the start date in order to pull off such a project.

This is the process that should trigger the red flags to go up if a due date is reasonable or not. If a large Wi-Fi project is due in three months, and the typical RFP process takes eight weeks before even awarding the contract, half the time will be elapsed before board approval and contracts can be executed. What if the signing authority is on vacation? What if there is an availability issue with the antennas? This project is doomed to fail.

Using MS Project, durations are entered into the DURATION column in the default form of five-day weeks. The planner can modify this default to include weekends and holidays as needed. This is one of the immediate and valuable aspects of this tool as it provides direct graphical feedback of timescales and schedules versus other possible tools like MS Word Tables or MS Excel. Task management tools will help sequence tasks and activities but don't give the overall project timeline in viewable format. MS Visio timelines are able to compute and display timelines in a very attractive manner but don't provide the flexibility to display simultaneous and overlapping tasks as well as MS Project.

Define Dependencies

Assigning predecessors in MS Project can be an exercise in arbitrary sequencing, or a true analysis of dependencies. The task predecessor becomes the key to triggering the task event. The PM should pay close attention if the predecessor is truly the task or milestone to initiate the subsequent task. Sometimes PMs using these tools simply line up tasks in order and assign predecessors in order to achieve a graphical representation of the order of tasks. However, if the PM takes the time and due diligence to assign predecessors based on actual task dependencies, then the project plan becomes a true planning and tracking mechanism, which can also be displayed as a critical path network diagram that can be used to understand task interdependencies.

For instance, in the Wi-Fi deployment that may take several weeks (or even months for a large school district), the task of verification testing should not follow the task of all site installations. Rather, the verification testing can be done for each site as it is completed. Therefore, the task of verification testing on the Gantt chart would match the duration and lag in completion by the time it takes to complete one site. This overlapping of tasks and dependencies is illustrated in figure 2.6—"Overlapping Timelines."

Multiple Dependencies

Often, and usually nearing the end of execution and project closeout, individual tasks have multiple dependencies. If tasks in sequence are each solely

Task Name	Duration	Start	Finish	Predecessors
- WiFi Project	20 days	Wed 10/18/17	Tue 11/14/17	
Fiber Optic BackBone	10 days	Wed 10/18/17	Tue 10/31/17	
Copper Horizontal Cabling	10 days	Wed 10/25/17	Tue 11/7/17	2FS-5 days
Verification Testing	10 days	Wed 11/1/17	Tue 11/14/17	3FS-5 days,2

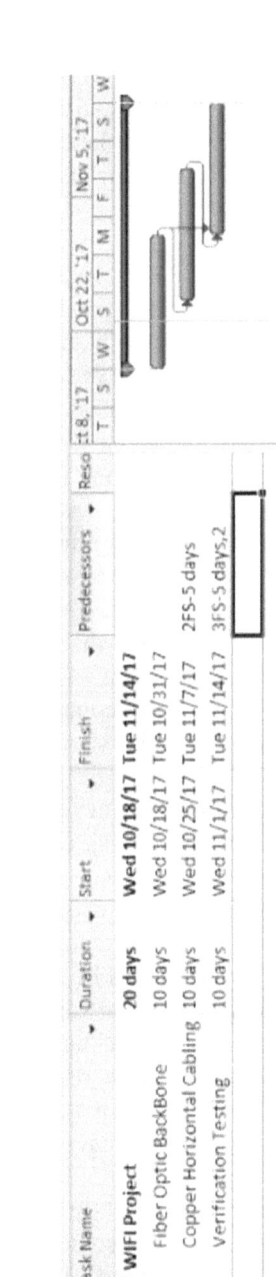

Figure 2.6 Overlapping Timelines

dependent on the previous task, then it is unnecessary to detail or display that a particular task has multiple dependencies. This is more for tasks reliant on unrelated projects. For instance, the Wi-Fi timeline in figure 2.6—"Overlapping Timelines"—the Verification Testing has an additional dependency of the Fiber Optic Backbone to be complete and the Copper Horizontal Cabling to be complete before the Verification Testing can begin.

Arrange Task Sequence

This process has already been initiated during task definition and task durations. Unless you think backward, it is most likely that you developed task definitions and durations in the general order of logical sequence, planning, infrastructure, acquisition, and execution. But as the PM drills deeper into each task and subproject, the ordering of tasks and dependencies is challenged by how they were initially defined, and how their true dependencies and hard schedule dates dictate. Meaning that arbitrary assignments of dependencies (predecessors in MS Project) can significantly impact project timelines.

At this point in the task sequencing, the PM must discriminate between true and arbitrary dependencies. For instance, even though power and rack requirements are lower-level infrastructure than structured cabling, that doesn't necessarily mean that the installation of structured cabling cannot proceed without the power upgrades. They could be done simultaneously. The equipment installation, however, cannot start until both are completed, no matter which begins first.

Similarly in the LMS scenario, professional development teacher training is not necessarily dependent on the actual licensing of the software, but training the teachers on software that they don't have access to immediately can prove ineffective and is an bad judgmental call. In the end, sequencing and dependencies may fall by the wayside to other external scheduling factors, like if funds aren't available until July 1, or if a facility will be closed for spring break.

In the LMS scenario, and almost any software rollout, training and/or professional development is dependent on technology equipment, software, training windows of opportunity (in service or prep days), and training resources. How often has a teacher received a training during a presession Professional Development (PD) day, only to have to wait for months, or for the availability of equipment?

Various training models can also significantly impact a software rollout. Models that can happen over time and using some sort of leveraged training model such as train-the-trainer, or site-based mentors/coaches, can make the implementation more cost-effective and effective overall. Figure 2.7—"LMS Rollout"—illustrates how the train-the-trainer phase is dependent on acquisition of the training devices and the licensing of the software.

Task	Duration	Start	Finish	Predecessors
LMS Rollout	37 days	Wed 11/15/17	Thu 1/4/18	
Procure Training Devices	5 days	Wed 11/15/17	Tue 11/21/17	4
Procure Devices	15 days	Wed 11/15/17	Tue 12/5/17	4
Software Licensing	5 days	Wed 11/15/17	Tue 11/21/17	4
Train the Trainers	2 days	Wed 11/22/17	Thu 11/23/17	8,10
Train the Teachers	30 days	Fri 11/24/17	Thu 1/4/18	11

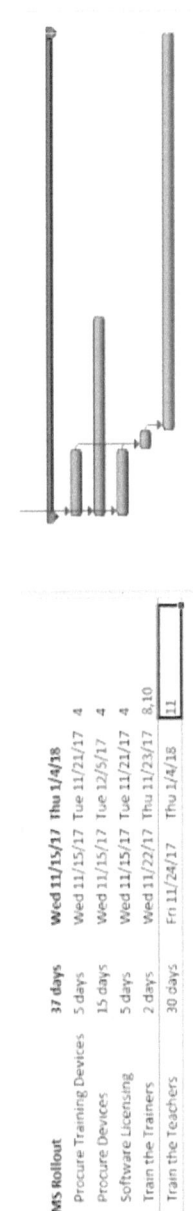

Figure 2.7 LMS Rollout Schedule

Resource Staffing

Define planning resources.

Define execution resources.

Define support resources.

Define escalation resources.

Define resource start and durations.

Figure 2.8   Resource Staffing

RESOURCE STAFFING

Once again, the early process of Task Definitions likely shed much light onto the resource staffing details of the plan. The inputs to this process are the Task Definitions and the Task Sequencing. This process of detailing resource staffing will require the granular details of who and when. Figure 2.8—"Resource Staffing"—details the steps in defining resource types, their start dates and durations.

Define Planning Resources

Planning resources are the in-house staff, SMEs, and stakeholders who are *required* for project planning. The reason the word "required" is italicized is because this is not a kick-off meeting where the PM is trying to build credibility and introduce the process. The planning resources are the actual parties who truly understand and will help dictate and decide how the project will proceed. The PM is the leader of the planning process, and he or she should be very careful about selecting planning resources. Even though this is an action-oriented group, and not "just-for-show," neglecting to include particular stakeholders can cause dissension or feelings of exclusion. The PM must work with his or her client stakeholders to engage the important planning resources and exclude dissenters and nonresources.

Additionally, the PM must recognize the difference between a planning resource and an execution (or implementation) resource. In the Wi-Fi scenario, the planning resource might be the IT director while the execution resource might be the network engineer. Or alternately, the IT director might say, the network engineer is the one who knows what, how, and how long for a particular task. This would indicate that the network engineer may need to be a planning resource. The next question would follow: Is the IT director a planning resource or simply a stakeholder?

In the LMS deployment scenario, the LMS company account manager might be the planning resource, although he or she will likely have to refer back to the LMS company's training provider, the real execution (training) resource.

PM Perspective

Again, it is important for the PM to keep feathers smoothed through this initial planning process as it is never helpful to create friction or feelings of exclusion for team members. However, these concerns must also be balanced with the actual client's objectives. This means that I always let the actual client make the call on political or hot-button issues. Who is the actual client? He (or she) is the one who actually engaged the PM and signs the checks (approves the invoices). In IT departments there are often strong opinions about the way things are done, will be done, and have been done in the past. If these opinions are held by individuals who may not be SMEs or execution resources, then their involvement may not be needed or may not even be constructive. Think of the begrudged network engineer who believes that student devices shouldn't have Internet access or that teachers and staff shouldn't have admin rights over their devices.

These types of "team" members should be excluded from action-oriented planning meetings under the direction of the IT director. Some stakeholders think they are SMEs or planning resources when they really aren't. Think about it.

The board member "wants to be involved" throughout the process and then becomes an obstacle because of unavailability or lack of response. As a caveat, the PM might err on the side of inclusion for stakeholders and then let them opt out of the detail-oriented planning meetings. Worse case, have the client give the uninvitation, best to keep the PM's nose out of district politics.

Define Execution Resources

As stated, execution resources are likely not the same as planning resources. Table 2.9—"Planning and Execution Resources"—details how they may differ or be the same.

Define Support Resources

Who are the support resources? These are critical staff who aren't planning or execution resources but may be SMEs or other resources key to the project. Support resources may be involved in logistics, location access, security, or authorizations. For instance, a custodian who holds the keys to all the IDFs at a particular school site might be a critical support resource but not an essential member of the planning or deployment team.

58   Chapter 2

Table 2.9 Planning and Execution Resources

Project	Planning Resources	Execution Resources
Wi-Fi installation	• IT director • Facilities director • Cabling contractor • PM • Network engineer	• Facilities department • Network engineer • Cabling contractor • PM
VoIP upgrade	• IT director • VoIP engineer (district) • Cabling contractor • PM • Network engineer	• VoIP vendor • VoIP engineer (district) • Network engineer • PM
LMS deployment	• Ed tech director • IT director • LMS vendor • PM	• PM • LMS vendor • Professional development and training
Classroom technology	• Ed tech director • IT director • Facilities director • PM	• Vendor • PM • Facilities inspector

Another example of a support resource would be an administrator who must provide permission to access a secure location. Simply by asking the question, "who else will be critical for execution," will help to identify support resources.

Define Escalation Resources

Escalation resources are the next level of support beyond the project execution and support resources. Basically they're the third rung up the ladder of support. For instance, if in the VoIP project, the vendor engineer is the execution resource for the QOS configuration, and the network guy from the district IT department is the support resource, then the manufacturer's helpline might be the escalation resource—the person the vendor engineer would call if he or she has a problem.

The escalation resource is almost always a technical or administrative resource outside of the project team. Because of this, these resources should be informed of their inclusion in the project planning phase and that they are being identified as an escalation resource. Nothing like getting a support call from someone you don't even know. The PM should consider if any of the escalation resources should also be included in the communications plan. This will be considered later when support processes are defined.

The escalation resource is often the only other resource you can think of that may be able to help, the manufacturer's helpline is often the default, but you better verify that it works or that it is paid for, before you write it in your project escalation plan.

Define Resource Start and Durations

Each resource must be engaged through the duration of his or her project involvement. That means that the project manager must define the resource start date and duration, but in addition to the definition, there may be critical requests or contracts required to engage those resources, and this may cost money and require approvals.

For instance, if an IT department resource will be required for the planning and execution phases, then not only must the PM review these timelines with that resource and their management, but he or she must also check for contingencies like training, vacations, and planned events. Often, it is not until the PM has requested the resource to book the dates that these scheduled events may have real-world conflicts that must be resolved.

Consider the example of the timeline developed in the planning stages of the project. There may be an execution resource that is scheduled months down the line. If this particular resource doesn't book the project into his or her calendar, he or she may accidently plan a trip to Australia over the event. Then what? The PM may need to reengage with another resource or even pay a consulting resource to fill that need. That engagement may cost money and need additional approvals.

So not only must the PM release the timelines but also seriously engage the planning and execution resources and get sound commitments for the execution time frames and engagements. If third parties are involved, then these quotes and purchase orders must be initiated and processed weeks before the actual deployment. What if a specialized Wi-Fi engineer is required for project execution but the purchase order for his or her execution engagement isn't processed in time? Does it need to be approved by the board?

This can cause massive delays if details like this are not foreseen and planned. Most viable integration companies will not even schedule a resource without a purchase order. Worse yet, many high-level resources will book out, meaning their next window of availability may be next week, next month, or in six months.

SCHEDULE DEVELOPMENT

Schedule development is when the actual plan timeline starts to take shape. Once again, if MS Project is the tool, the PM should maximize the capabilities of the software as its Gantt chart, Critical Path, Resource

Schedule Development

Create master project schedule.

Sub project schedules.

Coordinate resource schedules.

Develop assumptions and requirements.

Figure 2.9   Schedule Development

Assignments, and Tracking Gantt charts are valuable tools for project planning as well as management (these are very different uses of the software). Figure 2.9—"Schedule Development"—details the process of developing the project schedule based on resource schedules and assumptions.

There is a big difference between using MS Project for planning versus project management. For planning it creates an excellent graphical depiction (Gantt chart) of the project timeline and task interdependencies. However, if not used correctly, the chart can be more of a pain and hindrance. A good PM doesn't need a PM tool to track tasks and resources—it can be done successfully with a notepad and discipline. So the PM must decide if the MS Project plan is also used as a tracking tool in the project execution phase.

Oftentimes, the Gantt chart goes by the wayside during execution because so many other documents, communications, and activities are ongoing that the need to view them within a tracking Gantt chart takes more work than needed to just keep tasks supported and status reported. There will be much more discussion about execution in the next chapter.

Create Master Project Schedule

As the timeline and project schedule are created, the tool once again becomes a focal point. Whether using MS Project, MS Excel, MS Word, or a bevy of other available tools, the most powerful feature must be the ability to create hierarchical levels that can be expanded and collapsed. MS Word Outline Mode or other outlining software is perfect for this application, but keep in mind, even sticky notes will work, so don't get bogged down by identifying this tool.

One of the most fundamental yet challenging concepts for creating a project plan is selecting the start date. The project start date becomes the critical date that all planning is based on, yet the decision must be made weeks, months, or even years before actual implementation begins, so which start date are we talking about? The project start date or the planning start date? The planning start date is now? But is there a known project start date?

First, let's define some "start" dates. There's the contract award, the project kick-off, the planning start date, the procurement start date, and the implementation (execution) start date. In a regular private-sector IT project, there is often the luxury of forward planning, meaning that everything is based on an initial start date, and sequenced forward. There are, however, several reasons that a project is planned in reverse, meaning that everything is based on a delivery date, such as a new law taking effect, or construction- or facilities-driven timelines. There can also be external factors such as weather or holidays that factor into scheduling.

In schools there are several educational factors that could drive scheduling like summer breaks, in-service days (for training), new school years, and winter breaks. These become important factors for cutovers and downtime. When using a tool such as MS Project, it would not be uncommon to start a project the day you create the new file. But ultimately, a real start date should be based on a milestone or event—namely, the kick-off meeting. Once the kick-off meeting is scheduled and accepted by the stakeholders, the planning process can then be based off this event. This should give the project planner/manager a couple of weeks lead time to develop and fine-tune the initial project schedule.

Almost every education technology or IT project will at the bare minimum have these milestones and start dates within the four basic milestones described earlier. Table 2.10—"Project Specific Milestones"—provides examples of typical milestones within each project phase.

Table 2.10 Project Specific Milestones

Milestone	
Project initiation	1. Award or contract execution
	2. Project kick-off
	3. Planning start date
Plan completion	4. Procurement start date
	5. Equipment acquisition
	6. Facilities provisioning
Execution completion	7. Asset inventory
	8. Preconfiguration
	9. Logistics
	10. Implementation/deployment/execution
Project completion	11. Verification testing/commissioning
	12. Knowledge transfer/training
	13. Acceptance

Starting with the initial milestone event, like the kick-off meeting, create the high-level project tasks and activities. As each is identified, assign durations and determine dependencies. Upon finishing the high-level outline headings, such as those detailed previously, expand on each subproject and subtasks. Be sure to assign predecessors based on real-world dependencies. For instance, just because the structured cabling installation is complete doesn't mean that the installation of switches can begin even if they haven't been ordered yet. Meaning that the switch procurement should start well before the structured cabling is completed, maybe even starting the procurements at the same time.

Create Subproject Schedules

Subprojects are smaller projects within bigger projects. For instance, structured cabling is almost always a subproject of any network, Wi-Fi or VoIP project. Remember the concept of progressive elaboration. At this point in the planning, the planner can simply allocate an expected amount of time for the subproject. Later, he or she will need to define all the tasks and activities within the subproject. The subproject may have all the milestones described earlier in the master schedule.

Subprojects may be too granular for the Gantt chart. A simple single-task item may represent another resource's whole scope of work for a duration. In the LMS deployment project, it would not be necessary for the phases of the server hardware upgrade subproject to be listed in the high-level Gantt chart. The task of "server provisioning" may be appropriate.

The VMware engineer, however, may require a 20-step script and escalation support in his or her version of the project plan. And while the actual work may only take one day, the preparation and scheduling with the vendor for custom configuration may take one or more weeks.

Coordinate Resource Schedules

Each resource may need a formal request, scope of work, or contract in order to lock in engagement. Many of these vehicles still require hard-copy requests and approvals, especially when going outside your organization. Also keep in mind that each project and subproject may require resources for both planning and execution. Ask the question, "What will it take to engage that resource?"

Resources designated as executive sponsor or internal resources might be able to simply add their scope to their schedule and confirm, or they might actually need to be relieved of other job responsibilities in order to be a resource for the project. This relief might require additional staffing or departmental cross-billing. Some of these types of commitment details may take days or even weeks to iron out.

For example, a past project that requires ADMIN access to a database application in order to implement a software module couldn't be resourced because the original software development company no longer existed. The IT director had to find another company familiar with the back-end system in order to "break-into" the production database application. This required a sales call, an assessment and a quotation for development services from an entirely new vendor, a process that took two additional weeks, and additional dollars not projected.

It is at this point of the planning process that the PM should begin asking resources about availability and engagement requirements—meaning that the PM should start communicating with resources and identifying the engagement vehicles. That means asking, "Will you be available at this time for this activity?" This question is rarely answered with a simple yes or no. Oftentimes, it must be qualified by availability and other projects and commitments. Internal resources may not offer any availability commitment without acknowledgment from their manager. Don't be surprised when each internal resource's answer is prefaced with "I'm so busy right now." And undoubtedly, each external resource will be ready, willing and able to provide quotations and scope(s) of work proposals.

To trigger these events, the PM can start by using e-mail to formalize each request. Once again, e-mailed requests are immediately memorialized, time stamped, and (usually) backed-up. This initial e-mail will provide the vehicle to initiate communications, provide project information and timelines relevant to the team and each resource, and provide the formalized request for each resource to check their calendar, get acknowledgment and approval, or provide a quote, depending on the engagement requirements. Table 2.11—"Engagement Requirements"—details how each resource for each project might need to be engaged for the project planning and/or execution.

Develop Assumptions and Requirements

Now that resources have been scheduled and their commitment formalized, this final task will detail the assumptions made for each resource engagement and the vehicles used to engage. What's the significance of this task? The assumptions may include important factors in the scheduling. For instance, the project may require the internal network engineer to support the implementation, but it is known that he or she is taking a three-week vacation late in the project. Any delays might cause the project to need him or her just as

64   Chapter 2

Table 2.11 Engagement Requirements

Project/Task	Resources	Engagement Requirements
Wi-Fi installation	IT director	Executive sponsor
	Facilities director	Internal resource
	Cabling contractor	Contract or purchase order
	Project manager	PM (internal resource or contract)
	Network engineer	Internal resource
VoIP upgrade	IT director	Executive sponsor
	VoIP engineer (district)	Internal resource
	VoIP engineer (vendor)	Contract or PO
	Cabling contractor	Contract or PO
	PM	PM (internal resource or contract)
	Network engineer	Internal resource
LMS deployment	Ed tech director	Executive sponsor
	IT director	Internal resource
	LMS vendor	Contract or purchase order
	PD staff	Internal resource
	PM	PM (internal resource or contract)
Classroom technology	Ed tech director	Executive sponsor
	IT director	Internal resource
	Facilities director	Internal resource
	PM	PM (internal resource or contract)
	Vendor	Contract or PO
	Facilities inspector	Contract or PO

he or she is leaving on vacation. Or, in terms of the engagement vehicle, what if the contract needs board approval and it didn't get on the board agenda? That would delay the resource at least two weeks.

PROJECT BUDGET

Project budgeting is much different from the ROM budgeting technique that was discussed in *FAIL TO PLAN, PLAN TO FAIL: MAPIT® Strategic Planning*, the prequel to this book. ROM budgeting is used to develop long-range and strategic plans.

They are typically used to prioritize initiatives, identify funding sources, strategize payouts and cash flow, and encumber funds. They allow large projects to be phased and prioritized. Project budgeting on the other hand requires much more accuracy and detail—project budgets are no longer "rough order magnitude." The project budget is used to identify cash flow availability and to set expectations with fiscal management of what expenditures are planned for a specific project and timeline.

Project budgets are used to encumber funds for near-term procurements and implementations. Project budgeting uses fewer contingencies and attempts to

Project Budget

Bill of materials.

Vendor / contractor services.

Recurring costs.

Planning / consulting services.

Procurements.

Figure 2.10 Project Budget

include all associated costs accurately. Think of the time a network upgrade needed more power outlets installed, or a bigger memory card. Or when the "enterprise" version of the software was $10,000 versus $500. This type of missed cost projection can stop a project in its tracks. Figure 2.10—"Project Budget"—lists the major components of the project budget.

Even though contingencies may have cast an umbrella over miscellaneous costs in the ROM budget, the project budget must include fact-based costs for every line item—and don't forget labor, local taxes, and shipping costs. Oh and waste disposal and recycling fees; oh and patch cords, both sides, and what color and length? Project budgets may include minute details such as multiyear licensing agreements, service and maintenance contracts, mounting brackets, and cable management (zip ties).

Imagine forgetting the patch cords and having to order several hundred of a specific type of fiber-patch cords for an upcoming installation. Worse yet imagine year-two after a network upgrade when the IT director receives a maintenance contract renewal for $20,000. All these costs should be included in the project budget, and all recurring costs should be highlighted to all those responsible for the project in the out years.

Bill(s) of Materials

Bill(s) of materials are one of the project planner's key tools in budget planning. By building a complete bill of materials, the planner attempts to cover all costs for equipment procurement. For complex technology projects, this would likely include labor and project management services.

Pricing estimates are best garnered from recent procurements by entities of similar size and type. Meaning that there's no telling what discount level your school would receive for any particular manufacturer's products. Oddly enough, the manufacturer's discounts off list can easily swing from 15% all the way to 70% or even 80% off manufacturer's suggested retail price (MSRP) depending on how large and strategic your district is to their quarterly goals. Unfortunately, the reality is that smaller school districts may never be able to access the deep discount levels of some of the top-tier school districts.

Just do a quick comparison by searching the Internet for products by part number. You'll see all the distributors offering the products at their "street price." These prices are typically in the range of 15% to 30% off MSRP and are standard discounts off list. Using the street price for project budgeting is a good way of staying on the outside of an estimate, while the MSRP is even more outside. The PM should be able to assume that the manufacturer would offer a greater discount on competitive bids, but this is not a general rule. Manufacturer's discounts and incentive programs may change from quarter to quarter and from reseller to reseller.

Creating bill(s) of materials estimates gets real tricky with large networking manufacturers like Cisco because there's no telling what new program or end of cycle promotions might be pending. Schools and other public agencies may share information from recent procurements to see what discount levels might be offered at any time, but there's really only one way to be sure to get the best price, and that is by doing a formal bid process.

We won't get into the laws of public contracting and state contracting codes in this book, but the major considerations of the project budgeting process are to closely estimate all associated procurements related to a project in order to provide leadership and stakeholders with an accurate estimate of how much a project will cost, in order for them to identify and encumber the funding.

PM Perspective

One thing the PM should know about this matter—provide and install type procurements of data communications and networking equipment (including Wi-Fi) is NOT construction or public works. Many of the restrictive rules and regulations regarding public contracting and public works do not apply to school technology projects. PMs should be aware of the limits and thresholds of the state contracting codes in order to avoid protests or misappropriation of funds.

Vendor/Contractor Services

Services estimates for vendor or contractor services can become the big question mark in your project budget. There is no way to know how one vendor will estimate resources and cost versus another. Some vendors might have unit pricing for installation and engineering tasks. For example, imaging a laptop with 25 applications might be $50, or configuring and installation of an edge switch might take a half-hour of preconfiguration (off premises) and one hour onsite installation.

Once again, recent procurements of similar size and scope can be used to guesstimate this budget number. The PM must be advised, however, if it's not in the vendor's scope of work, it's not in his cost proposal either. If the client comes back after the project has been awarded and asks for configuration (engineering services), you can bet it won't be for free.

Recurring Costs

With hosting, voice, and data network services all going to the cloud, more and more capitalized costs are moving to the expense side of the financials. The result is a larger percentage of dollars going toward recurring cost. Of course, some public monies are one-time or nondiscretionary, meaning that they can only be used certain ways, but the more costs move to the expense model, the more difficult it is to plan and budget large-scale procurements.

The PM can normalize some of these costs by stipulating multiyear agreements or life cycles in order to fund annualized or monthly recurring costs. Also purchasing five-year or lifetime warranties on critical components can help with life cycle costs. The last thing the PM wants to do is build a budget and not inform the owner about recurring costs that will blow their out-year operating budget.

For instance, an IT department's operating budget may not be able to support a large-scale maintenance contract in year-two after installation. This situation can leave a production network without manufacturer's support when it's most needed.

Services such as telecommunications, hosting, and XaaS (X as a Service) typically have monthly or annual licensing. Be sure to have complete life cycle costs, including growth, escalation, and inflation built realistically into the project budget, and have recurring costs highlighted in all the project documentation.

Planning/Consulting Services

The PM is best advised to include the costs of project planners and project managers if these skills or roles are out of the scope of the PM. For instance, in a larger Wi-Fi project, the PM may elect to engage a construction manager to oversee the structured cabling subproject.

In the development of any project budget, it's likely that planning and PM fees are already accounted for, but the following phases or projects that require planning and project management should also be well documented and communicated to the owner/client. The PM should also consider that the vendor or contractor's PM is not representing the client's best interest before their own. That means the school MUST have its own PM regardless of how many other PMs are assigned by vendors, contractors, or third parties.

Approvals

Approvals, both tacit, and formal, are required at EVERY decision point of a project. The more the PM can get approvals, the better. Any decision made without follow-up confirmation is subject to being presumptive or taking liberties. The PM must be disciplined in not making decisions in a vacuum, and if he or she does, he or she should seek immediate confirmation.

The PM must also recognize that his or her client and primary contact may not be the only approval required. For instance, if a consensus has been reached on a specific network architecture and configuration, the business director may not be the most important approval required. The IT director and the network engineer should also be in the approval chain.

The planner and PM should identify milestones for formal approvals. Table 2.12—"Approval Milestones"—details the most likely milestones for most projects and the manner or vehicle used.

Procurements

Procurements are the initial components of execution. This part of the project budget will identify and accumulate the procurements required to initiate the implementation phase of the project. With many projects there will be several procurements. The largest of the procurements will typically require a formal

Table 2.12 Approval Milestones

Milestone	Approval	Vehicle
Project award	Formal	Contract, purchase order, or notice to proceed (NTP)
Project kick-off	Formal	Scheduled meeting
Implementation plan	Informal	Plan delivery and review
Execution phase	Formal	Contract, PO, or NTP
Phase or subproject completion	Formal	Acceptance/conditional acceptance
Verification testing	Formal	Test results
Knowledge transfer	Informal	Training materials
Project completion	Formal	Acceptance document

bidding process, which in turn requires an RFP. The smaller procurements may be initiated with purchase orders, informal bids, or change orders.

RFPs require either generalized "performance specifications" or "specific" bills of materials, including manufacturers' part numbers if possible. Performance specified bids are used for "open" bids where various manufacturers' equipment or solution architectures are NOT predetermined and the manufacturers are to propose their best solutions based on the performance requirements. Specified manufacturers' bills of materials or RFPs specifying part numbers typically require the RFP to allow for "or equal" parts and equipment in order to render the bid "open."

State contracting codes differ, but typically, a public agency cannot purchase specific manufacturer's equipment without a competitively negotiated bid—meaning that if the manufacturer is specified, there must be an "or equal" provision in the bid. Sole-source agreements may come into play for some manufacturers like Apple, but for the most part, proprietary systems can still be competitively bid through different resellers allowing schools to still attempt to get the best price through a competitive bid process.

One way to avoid the open bid process would be to utilize a previously competitively bid contract vehicle such as a state award schedule or a consortium bid that allows an agency to "piggy-back" their public bid results. These schedules or prenegotiated agreements, however, are rarely the best attainable price—they are typically closer to what's known as "street price."

Another way to avoid the bid process would be if the equipment is a district-approved standard. This usually means board approval—such as standard for IBM computers and Cisco networking equipment. It is rare for a school district to approve a standard for such things as firewalls, or software applications; however, a district standard for Google Classroom or Microsoft 365 might be appropriate.

There are many facets to these large-scale procurements, but suffice it to say that manufacturers will not be incented to provide discounted rates if they are not in competition. Similarly, if bidders know all their competitors and their pricing, they will not be incented to discount their profit margins beyond these known thresholds. If it is the client or district's goal to get the best price for large-scale procurements, and as an agency expending public funds it certainly should be, the formal competitive bid process (RFP) is still the best way to get the best price.

The total of all the bill(s) of materials, contractor services, recurring costs, planning and consulting services, and procurements (bills of material may be encompassed within the procurements) will be summarized in the project budget. This budget will initially be used to qualify each component and identify and encumber funds. The budget should be memorialized as "Budget & Date" and kept as a metric through project execution. As actual expenditures are made, a tracking budget should be maintained to provide a cost comparison between the budget and actual costs. This may be a key to identifying a cost overrun, which would trigger a risk assessment.

PLAN DEVELOPMENT

The final phase of project planning and the preparation of all the documents and materials to begin execution are compiled in the project plan. The project plan may consist of many different items including:

1. Plan narrative
2. Assumptions
3. Vendor/contractor/client responsibilities
4. Logical designs and system architectures
5. Physical layouts
6. Implementation plan—tasks and activities
7. Project budget
8. Implementation timeline

Gantt Chart

Although it has been discussed here many times, the Gantt chart is still probably the best overall tool for presentation of an implementation timeline. Where the implementation plan might be a document with tables and dates, the Gantt chart provides that great high-level graphic that allows resources and stakeholders alike to "ohh" and "ahh" about something that actually makes sense.

Whether they truly understand the critical path and interdependencies, most will be able to identify the beginning and end dates to see when the project should be complete and get a high-level understanding of the project phases. Whether the Gantt chart is maintained as a tracking Gantt chart during execution is another story. But as a key plan deliverable, it is a critical component. Figure 2.11—"Gantt Chart"—shows a typical education technology gantt chart created using MS Project.

Key Components to the Gantt Chart

Every Gantt chart should at minimum detail the following tasks and/or activities and milestones:

- Project start date—Kick-off meeting
- Project planning phase

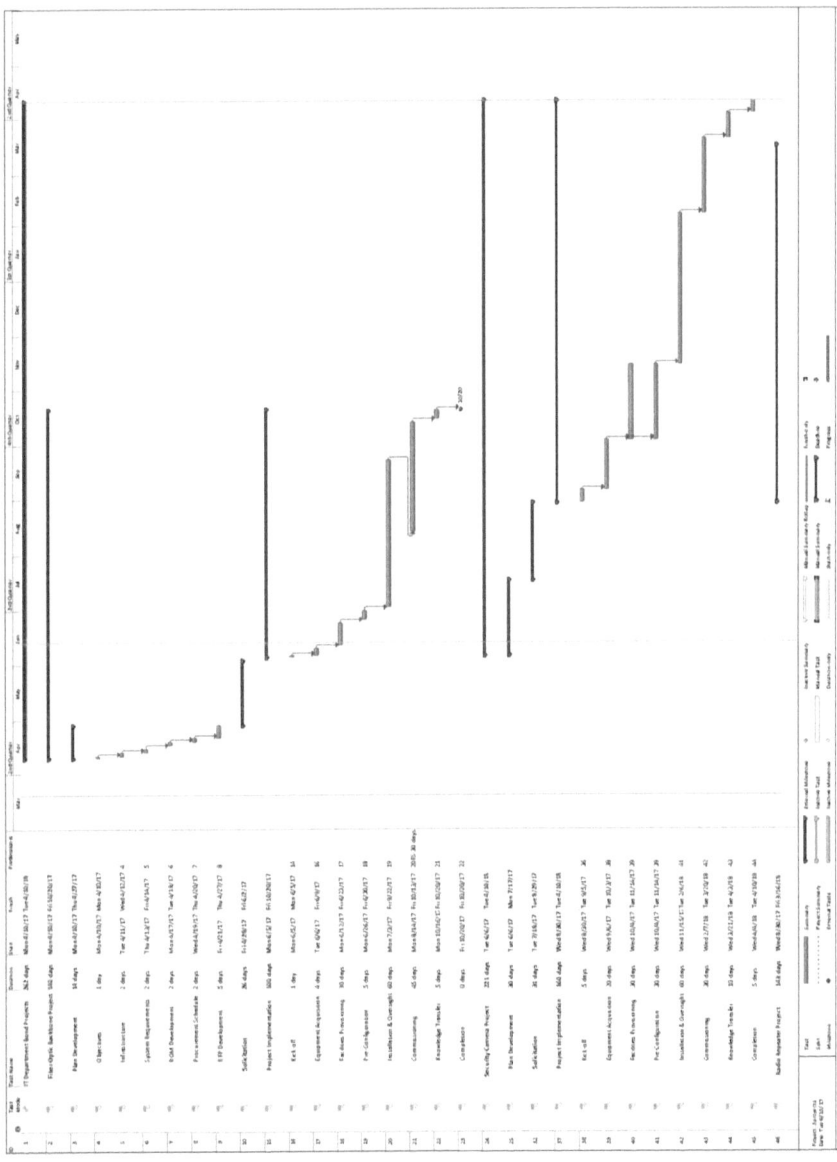

Figure 2.11 Gantt Chart

- Project execution phase
- Project completion date
- Task interdependencies (predecessors)
- Resources

The Gantt chart is an excellent way to communicate a project timeline but not the only way. MS Excel spreadsheets or MS Word tables can also be used to generate logical sequential timelines, although MS Project does the best job at showing dependencies and allows the generation of other chart types automatically; the most common secondary chart is the critical path chart also known as a Network Diagram.

If the Gantt chart is solely for formal plan presentation, MS Visio has excellent project timeline and Gantt chart tools that allow importing and synchronization. The date and duration features work nicely to automatically adjust just by stretching the objects. Oftentimes, MS Project timelines can get too detailed and busy, and a more graphically pleasing and less detailed timeline is needed to communicate generalized timelines and milestones. These types of graphical timelines are better suited for formal and executive level presentations. Figure 2.12—"MS Visio Timeline"—illustrates how a more graphically pleasing Gantt Chart can be created using MS Visio.

It was discussed earlier that Gantt charts can also be used to track progress during execution, but the question must be asked: Who is going to look at this tracking Gantt chart? If the answer is no one, then the time and effort required to maintain this chart may not be worth it. Figure 2.13—"MS Visio Tracking Timeline"—shows how a tracking Gantt Chart compares a project plan with actual elapsed times.

On the other hand, if stakeholders are expecting this type of project tracking update each week, and the tracking Gantt chart is the easiest way to convey the objective each week, then the tracking Gantt chart becomes the key focus for status reporting. It is not uncommon to abandon the Gantt chart once actual project execution is underway because there are too many other real tasks and activities to be managed and maintained and other documents to manage these tasks and activities.

One of the reasons the tracking Gantt chart becomes unwieldy is because status reports require much more unstructured communication, such as update reports, progress statements, milestones, and related descriptions that don't have a place in a Gantt chart. For this reason, the weekly status report best remains a MS Word or Google document, or even an e-mail (formatted correctly for status reporting, of course). Informal updates via e-mail with inconsistent formatting, update information, or distribution lists should not take the place of a formal weekly status report. Remember the axiom, "informal is irrelevant."

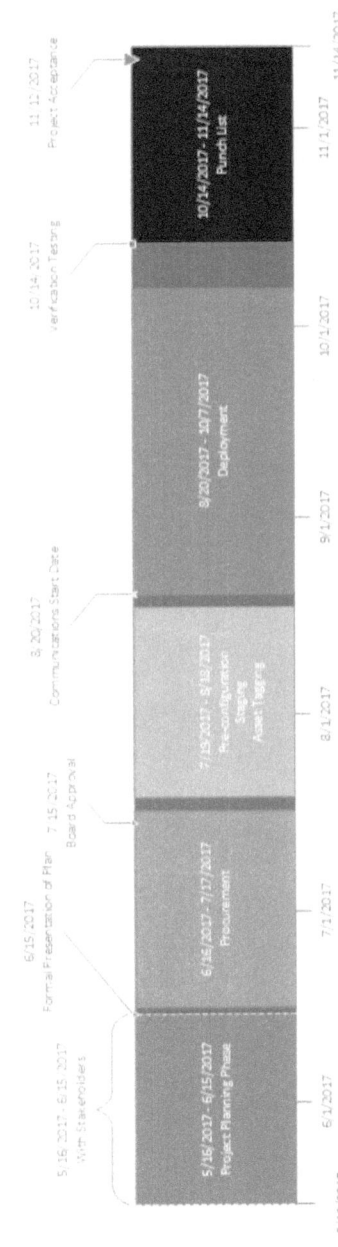

Figure 2.12 MS Visio Timeline

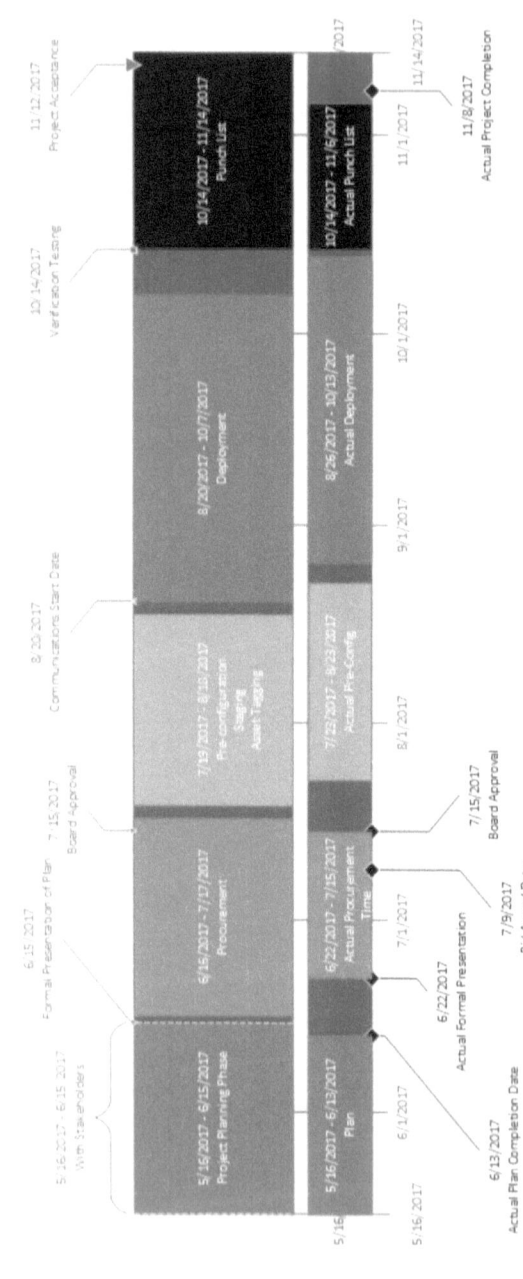

Figure 2.13   MS Visio Tracking Timeline

Project Kick-Off

Scheduling the project kick-off is the milestone that officially starts the project in the world's view. Unlike a strategic plan, a project kick-off need not be a ceremonious event—it simply needs to engage resources and initiate the planning process. This usually means a contract or approval of some sort. If the planner is an outside resource, then a contract for consultant services is likely required. If an internal resource, then an approval from the planner's direct manager would be the required approval. The PM must be empowered with authority and ability to engage resources based on the project objectives. Without this autonomy and authority, the PM can be rendered powerless and unsuccessful. By successfully scheduling and executing the project kick-off, the endeavor becomes official and the project clock starts ticking.

Support Processes

It is at this phase of the plan development that the MAPIT® support processes will come to center stage. All of chapter 3 is dedicated to the support processes and, like any plan, should be scaled according to the project. There are seven plans that comprise the MAPIT® support processes, but for smaller projects, each plan might be a one-page document or even a paragraph in the overall plan. Two particular support processes should always be present in any project: the communications plan and the change management plan.

The communications plan will become one of the project plan deliverables. It will define all project communications, the method, frequency, and distribution lists. Other items might also be addressed in a comprehensive communications plan such as specific project milestones and look-ahead reports.

The change management plan must detail how the PM and project team will deal with changes to the plan and execution. This really becomes a matter of how the main client/owner wants to deal with project changes. For smaller projects, a simple flowchart and understanding might do the job, but for large, complex projects, changes are usually associated with impacts to one of the triple constraints. If there is a risk to one of the triple constraints, that would trigger the risk management plan, the third most critical support process.

It is the risk management plan that provides the process of identifying new information that impacts one of the constraints and sets the plan into motion. It is the outcome of the risk management plan that typically triggers the change management plan, although, as will be detailed, it is possible to engage change management without risk management.

PM Perspective

It is during the final plan development that the PM will determine the relevant plans and their scope and details. For instance, for a small wireless implementation project at an individual school site, the resource staffing plan would just be to use in-house resources. The change management plan would be to handle any difficult installations individually. And the communications plan would be a weekly status report, punch list, and as-built documentation. The next chapter—"Support Processes"—will go in depth into each of these plans.

Chapter 3

Support Processes

MAPIT® support processes are the plans and procedures used to manage resources, communications, changes, risks, data integrity, and overall project quality, through the project execution and project completion phases. Each process, defined in the planning phase, will become an operational process in the project execution phase and comprise the core of project management. So where the core processes support project planning, the support processes support project management. Figure 3.1—"Support Processes"—details the seven support processes.

It's duly noted that some of the support processes, such as change management and risk management, may bounce the PM back into revisions of the original project plan. So with the wisdom imparted that documents shouldn't be living documents, each revision to the original project plan should be considered a new project plan, with new dates, milestones, and targets, and all efforts must be made to communicate this plan change or revision to resources and stakeholders—because those who aren't effectively communicated to about these changes will surely notice when their plans are negatively impacted by your project change.

As stated, a small project may not require all the support process plans, and the ones it does require may be very simple. However, the larger the project (more money), the more critical the need for each plan. This chapter—Support Processes—takes on two perspectives, first to provide the reader with the format and method for identifying the relevant plans (all are relevant except in the smallest projects) and second as a process and procedure to support project execution—or *how to use the support processes for project management*.

The reader is challenged to absorb this chapter twice—in the first reading to understand the scope and purpose of each of the support processes, and in

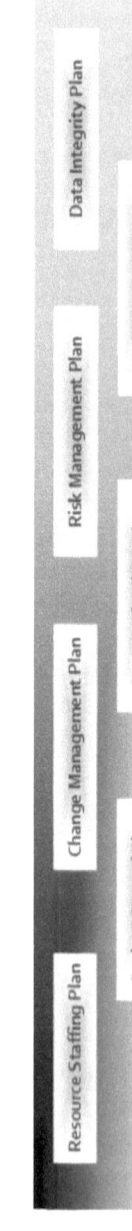

Figure 3.1 **Support Processes**

the second reading to aid in the development and implementation of each plan using the included templates. Once defined, the PM will utilize each plan during project execution. For this reason, it becomes clear that these plans must be defined, published, and distributed BEFORE project execution begins.

In fact, they should be part of the project plan to be approved by the client, resources, and stakeholders before funding. It is not appropriate to be in the middle of project execution and proclaim a data integrity plan is in effect without ever mentioning it during the planning phase, or to make changes to a resources scope because of a quality assurance plan that the resource doesn't know about. So, there is a section in each project plan that defines and explains each support process.

COMMUNICATIONS PLAN

The communications plan is likely the most important of the support processes. Every project must have a communications plan. The communications plan can make the difference between a successful project or a disaster, even if the outcome is the same. For example, a core LAN upgrade that will cause a four-hour outage at minimum could have two separate outcomes:

1. The PM communicates that a minimum eight-hour outage will occur over a weekend in the future, and the cutover goes as planned with no users impacted—success!
2. The PM doesn't communicate the outage and attempts to do the cutover at lunch on a Friday that results in a four-hour outage—disaster!

Same downtime but without effective communication, this disaster could have been mitigated. The communications plan would have required that the downtime include a request and approval process from all possible impacted departments. With a possible downtime of up to four hours, the likelihood of getting approval to implement this upgrade during a lunch hour, no matter how confident the engineers are, is nil. And for good reason, when was the last time a network engineer correctly estimated the possible downtime and complexity of a network upgrade? The engineer might be the SME, but the PM would take the estimate and double the execution time and possibly triple the projected downtime estimate.

Of course, there are a number of other scenarios that could result, but the point is that even a disaster can be mitigated simply by forewarning users about an outage long beforehand and setting expectations planning for the worst-case scenario. In a mission critical situation, these types of outages not only need to be communicated but also approved by all potentially impacted user groups.

The communications plan will include the communication type (memo, status, timeline), the mode (verbal, written, meeting), the frequency (daily, weekly, monthly), and the distribution list. Stating in the communications plan that a particular communication will occur on a certain frequency will establish a base-level expectation for communications. It will be contingent upon the PM to follow through—making the communications plan not only a tool for standardizing communication modes and frequency but also as a noose to hang himself or herself with if he or she doesn't follow through with his or her stated commitments—in essence, the communications plan is also a litmus test of the PM's discipline in process and procedure.

The communications plan will demonstrate if the PM is a man (or woman) of their word. Oftentimes, the PM's discipline in keeping to these communication plans truly tests the mettle of the PM. Thus, the PM must strike a balance between what is necessary to keep the stakeholders appraised and up to date and what is too much to keep up with along with the other PM tasks at hand.

Defining too much formal communication can not only be too much work for the PM but will also get ignored as too much information. However, it is always better to be blamed for providing too much information than the opposite, and by doing so in the early stages may allow stakeholders to request less information. "Just send me the relevant project timelines" is a good form of feedback.

Utilizing e-mail is also an excellent method of communications because it is documented, time stamped, archived, and auditable. Using MS Word, Project, Visio, PowerPoint, or other tools for communications adds an extra layer of effort and review when important information can be communicated in the subject line of an e-mail, allowing stakeholders to quickly determine if the information is important for them.

The sample communications plan details how the communication type, method, and distribution list allow the PM to set expectations about how communications will be handled. The communications plan becomes a method to test various stakeholders about their level of interest and immersion in the project. Including more stakeholders in the distribution list of communications and then having them ask for less will always better.

PM Perspective

Even though status meetings may be part of the communications plan, status meetings by themselves can be a huge waste of time. Standing meetings with fixed participants can actually have the negative effect if the PM doesn't keep this meeting productive and progress seeking. A status meeting where everyone says that things are hunky-dory and doesn't really resolve conflicts and issues or keeps the project momentum actually costs an enormous amount of money—just add up the hourly rates of all the participants and you'll fall out of your chair.

Standing meetings should be minimized and optimized—meaning minimize the frequency and only involve key resources and stakeholders. In order for a status meeting, or any meeting for that matter, to be productive requires the PM to track action items, owners, and due dates.

Utilize electronic media (e-mail, shared documents, workflow) to keep resources and stakeholders appraised at each step. Table 3.1—"Communications Plan"—depicts a sample plan for a generic project.

PROJECT CONTROL PLAN

MAPIT® project control plan is focused on documentation of project milestones and control points. The project control plan will help identify key milestones and define their attributes. For instance, the kick-off meeting—does it require all stakeholders or just project resources? Who will provide client acceptance? And what determines the completion of knowledge transfer?

Almost all documents associated to the project can become a project control device. The PM must define and employ the minimal number of project controls to streamline the execution process without compromising the number and quality of formal milestones and control devices.

Equipment and services procured in support of a project also provide copious control documents such as quotes, bids, bills of materials (BOMs), and packing slips (receiving documents). The proof of purchase will become the control point for the beginning of the procurement process, such as signed contracts and purchase orders (POs). POs are a major project control document because POs cannot be issued without funding and approvals outside of the IT department. Larger procurements require requests for proposals (RFPs) and board approval.

On the other side of the procurement, the receipt and acceptance of equipment provide control documentation: bills of lading, receiving documentation from the warehouse, and asset tags provide reconcilable documents to the procurement documents. Invariably, the finance department will require an asset inventory listing of all capital equipment. It's always better to create these documents as part of the acquisition process than to go around tagging equipment and scanning serial numbers after the deployment.

Not all these documents are necessary for a project control plan. It really depends on the scale and complexity of the project. If it's simply a purchase and install project, then project control will simply be to reconcile the procurement documents with the receiving documents, asset tags, and sign-offs.

Table 3.1 Communications Plan

Report Date:
The following communications plan is submitted by Networld Solutions in order to formalize communications and reporting between all stakeholders of ABC Company and the NWS project staff. This communications plan is applicable to all verbal and written communications regarding the Blankety-blank-blank project beginning on date through date.

Stakeholders

Name	Title	Company	Phone	E-mail Address
I. M. Client	Director of IS	ABC Company	999-999-9999	Imclient@abcc.com
Your Name	Program Manager	NWS	619-874-0464	xxx@bcsolutions.com
Darryl Vidal	Vice President	NWS	619-874-0464	dvidal@bcsolutions.com

Reporting

Type	Method	Description	Distribution List	Frequency
Verbal	Phone or Face-to-Face	Program Manager will communicate daily status, issues and progress against work plan with Project Manager.	PM Client	Daily
Timesheets	Work Order System	Each engineer, consultant and/or project manager will submit weekly timesheets detailing the hours worked per day, and a description of activities.	PM, NWS Admin Client	Weekly
Status Report	Email	Program Manager will write a weekly status report detailing weekly activities, accomplishments, plans for the following week, and outstanding issues.	PM Client Resources	Weekly
Meeting	Word Document and Project Timeline	A standing weekly status meeting has been set for each Monday, 9:00 am, in the conference room to review the Status Report and timesheets.	PM PM Client	Weekly Mondays 9:00am

A larger scope and scale project may require timesheets, monthly cumulation reports, RFPs, contracts, POs, punch lists, and so on.

Using the four project phases to determine project controls is a good method. The salient point for the PM is to identify the most significant control points for the project phases. It may not be necessary to reconcile every patch cord in a network upgrade against the PO, but it will be necessary to know where $2,000 worth of extra fiber patch cords are if asked the question.

Other important project controls are timesheets or billing information. Of course, these are project tasks and activities reported to justify time and billing. These may be the most important project controls, and they should be established at the very beginning of the project. The client should be instructed exactly how the project status will be monitored and controlled week by week. Timesheets provide weekly (or other frequency) reporting of time for client approval. This is a weekly project control point that allows the client to monitor progress against billing on a week-by-week basis. For larger projects the frequency might be biweekly or monthly.

For instance, timesheets become a control point for documentation and acceptance of hours of work performed. This is a huge component of project progress payments and the ability to show client acceptance. If the client is signing off on weekly timesheets, then it will be difficult to argue that hours of work were not performed or delivered at a later date. Of course, hours of work performed do not directly correlate to deliverables and project success; they are just a memorial of the time spent by resources. It's definitely possible to have five guys on-site working and not complete a deployment for some other reason. So although the timesheets are a valid project control for resource hours of work performed, they do not validate anything concrete in terms of deliverables.

Figure 3.2—"Project Control Documents"—shows the type and frequency of some project control documents that occur in almost any IT project that includes equipment and installation.

Progress payments are another form of project control. As opposed to timesheets, that are directly related to resource time and billing, progress payments are tied to project percentage of completion—usually in increments, such as 25%, 50%, 75%, and 100% of project completion. This type of project control separates resource time from project status. This can be a double-edged sword. It requires that both parties agree on the milestones and/or methods to determine the percentage of project completion.

This may be easy—if there are four reports to be developed, then the completion of each report can signify 25% completion. Or if a project has four distinct phases (that are somewhat balanced in duration or resources), then each phase can signify a milestone. On the other hand, this method can also get out of control. For instance, if a milestone is determined as a marker for a

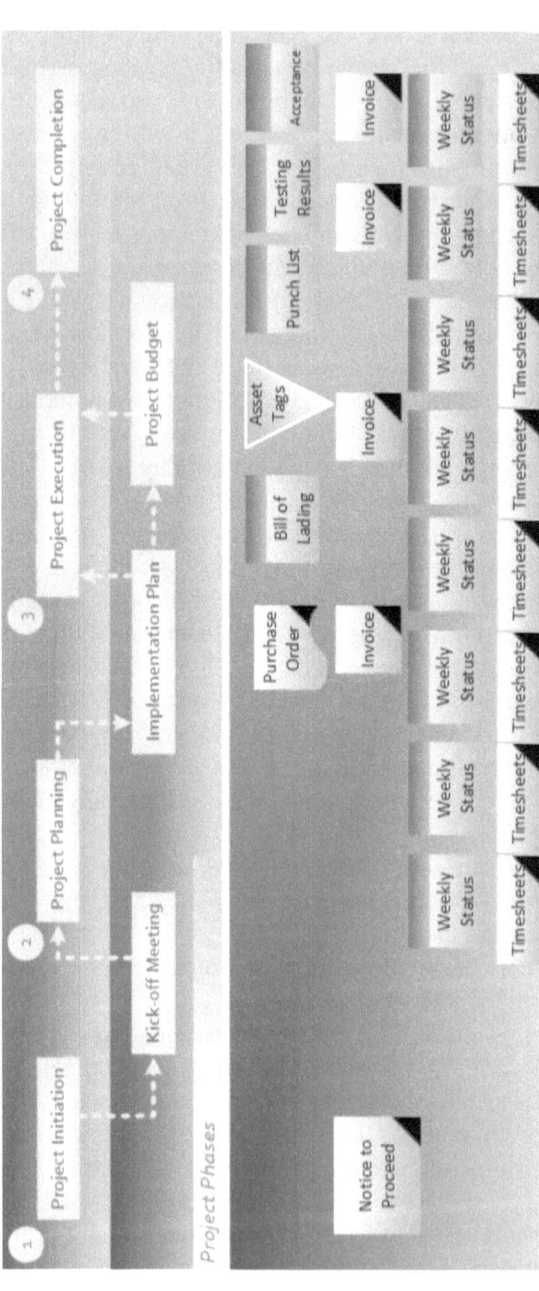

Figure 3.2　Project Control Documents

phase completion, but the client doesn't agree that the milestone has been reached, even if the resources and time elapsed have gone way beyond the percentage milestone, the parties may find themselves in a dispute.

Along with defining the key project milestones, the project control plan should also identify the key contacts for approvals, changes, and other project impacts. The following sample project control template (table 3.2) provides the table for developing a project control plan with associated sample data.

RESOURCE STAFFING PLAN

The support processes for resource staffing are focused on administration of project resources as opposed to "who and when." The "who and when" should have all been planned during the resource staffing plan development during the core planning processes. As a reminder, in that phase, the planner should have defined:

- Planning resources
- Execution resources
- Support resources
- Escalation resources
- Their start dates and duration

From a support process standpoint, the resource staffing plan should be able to trigger the necessary administrative functions to engage, report, and compensate resources (internal or external). Engagement might be in the form of a request to an internal resource via e-mail. For an external resource, this might be an informal request for a quote or bid. Compensation for internal resources may be a simple thank-you or possibly a department account code to charge against. Any external resource is going to need to be paid through an invoice and payment from the accounts payable department—which will likely require a PO number to reference.

In the core planning process, the resource staffing plan should have laid out the estimated planning and execution resources on a timeline or Gantt chart. Each resource will require an engagement vehicle or instrument, whether it be a contract, PO, or departmental approval, the resource must have a condition in process so that when the time comes, they are able to drop what they are doing and dedicate time to the project. So, once the resource staffing plan has been finalized and approved, the PM should begin engaging the planning and execution resources through administrative channels.

For instance, if a contract consultant will be used to help in design (planning) and configuration (execution), then the PM should request quotations or

Table 3.2 Project Control Template

Milestone/Action	Description	Example	Approval
Project initiation	Action that determines contractual start	Purchase order (PO) Notice to proceed (NTP) Signed contract	Purchasing Client
Project kick-off	Meeting of key project resources to initiate planning tasks and activities	Kick-off meeting Discovery interviews Communications e-mail	Client
Timesheets	Weekly timesheets detailing hours worked for each resource. Some may include task descriptions.	Vendor timesheet Monthly time and activities report	Client Supervisor
Invoices	Details about resources, hours, and descriptions allow client to monitor billing against project status.	Biweekly or monthly invoices	Client AP
Purchase orders	POs for equipment or services will need to be compiled and archived.	Equipment POs Service orders Requests for bids RFPs	Purchasing Client
Bills of lading	For actual equipment or products received. To be reconciled with POs	Receiving slips Packaging slips	Receiving clerks Purchasing
Asset tags	Tagged equipment and associated inventory database	Excel database: Part#, Serial #, Tag #	Finance
Verification testing	Results of any testing associated with project	Cat 6. cable tests Fiber OTDR tests Wireless heat map	IT department
Knowledge transfer	This usually consists of user orientation training specific to the installation, not formal training courses.	Systems documentation Manuals Processes and procedures	Operations staff Client
Training	Any type of formal training for users and administrators	Certifications	Project staff
Punch list	This is the final checkoff list of outstanding items.	Punch list Open items	Project staff Client
Final acceptance	Final signature of client acceptance	Final acceptance form	Client

proposals for the definitive amounts of time and resources necessary according to the scope. In an internal IT department resource, an e-mail formalizing the request may be all that is necessary, more likely in a for-profit organization, a charge number or billing account might be needed and approved.

PM Perspective

The PM should never assume that a simple e-mail request will be sufficient. In fact, the PM should verify the administrative process at the very beginning (planning stage). It's possible that an internal resource doesn't even know the administrative requirement for him or her to spend time on another scope of work. Table 3.3—"Resource Staffing Plan"—details how various resources may require a variety of engagement administration vehicles.

RISK MANAGEMENT PLAN

It is not relevant to designate which of the MAPIT® support processes is the most critical as we have already stated how important project controls and communications are critical to monitoring, reporting, and getting paid. But understanding RISK, and what to do when it is identified, becomes a critical skill for any PM.

Risk is when the PM identifies that one of the triple constraints is at risk of failure or negative impact. This is triggered by new information—information counter to or conflicting with planning estimates and assumptions. It is most important to note that every project encounters challenges and obstacles. The

Table 3.3 Resource Staffing Plan

Phase	Resource	Engagement	Administration Vehicle
Planning	Project manager	External contract	Purchase order
		Internal resource	Cost account
	Subject matter expert(s)	External contract	Purchase order
	Network design	Internal resource	Cost account
	Wireless design		Work order
Execution	Electrical contractor	External contract	PO or bid
	Network engineer	External contract	PO
		Internal resources	E-mail authorization from network manager
	Systems administrator—Wireless security	Internal resources	E-mail authorization from systems support manager
	Desktop technicians	Internal resources	E-mail authorization from help desk manager

planning process is designed to try to identify all the possible challenges and obstacles and address them in sequence in order to deliver the project on time and on budget.

In order to understand risk in the MAPIT® context, the PM must know:

- Definition of risk and risk factors
- How to identify scope risk factors
- How to identify budget risk factors
- How to identify time risk factors
- How to write a risk assessment report

First, a few definitions of risk management:

- (In business) the forecasting and evaluation of financial threats to the ongoing business concern together with the identification of procedures to avoid or minimize their impact (Wikipedia).
- (In ITIL) the forecasting of project triple constraint risks based on technology systems together with the procedures to identify, evaluate, and mitigate their impact.
- (In MAPIT® Project Management) the forecasting and monitoring of the three constraints in regards to their impact on project status and success.

The triple constraint in project management are these three factors: scope, time, budget (cost, resources). The key to risk management is risk IDENTIFICATION—knowing and having the intestinal fortitude to proclaim to the client, stakeholders, and resources that the project has an identified risk. New information impacting one or more of the triple constraints may trigger the risk management plan.

That is to assume that there is a risk management plan. As stated, this is one of the support processes that should be defined in the project planning process in order for the client and stakeholders to be familiar with the term and purpose for this plan. What is the purpose of the risk management plan? To address how risks will be assessed, reported, and mitigated.

It is also important to note that it is most common that risk to one of the constraints will likely affect the other constraints either directly or through mitigation. For instance, if a scope risk is encountered in the desktop deployment project, then the time constraint will be directly impacted unless some mitigation is implemented. If the client, through the risk assessment report, decides to add more resources to the deployment team, then both the scope and cost of the original plan will be revised and adjusted to keep the time constraint intact.

PM Perspectives

The PM must be very cognizant of any new information. New information doesn't typically march into the room proclaiming its impact. Sometimes the new information must be coaxed out of a resource or deduced from an e-mail or a conversation. The PM is advised that clients and resources don't want to be the bearer of bad news or in this case new information. Resources won't necessarily volunteer information that might brand them as the culprit for a missed deadline or cost overrun.

This is one reason the PM must have an intimate understanding of his or her resources and their relevance to the project phase. Meaning that once a salesperson makes the sale, he or she may no longer be the right source of information during the execution phase. As an example, when the sales representative says, "Oh yeah, everything is in stock right now." He or she might really mean, "I'll check and get back to you for real after I get the order."

Scope Risk Factors

Scope risk is any new information or project details that might force the scope of the project execution to include something that was not defined in the project plan. The example before in the Wi-Fi project would be if a few new cable drops are required but not included in the plan. This would trigger the need for a cable contractor, or in-house resources, to jump into action requiring additional resources, cost, and likely time.

Another example in the classroom technology project would be if the contractor's scope included removing old interactive whiteboards to be replaced with interactive screens. But after removing the old whiteboards, there was damaged or unpainted wall surfaces left exposed. Suddenly patching and painting of drywall becomes a part of the project and affects the scope and cost constraints (and probably time constraints as well). Not only that, but since the patching and painting are public works, now all the state codes and prevailing wage compliance laws are triggered.

"Scope creep" is a common term used to indicate that the scope of the project is growing beyond the initial project scope and plan. The key is in identification and declaration. If the PM ignores scope creep, the project scope could be at risk (or one of the other two constraints). Without specific acknowledgment the PM will not be able to keep the scope creep from causing the project to miss a due date or fail. The PM must declare the risk as early as possible because mitigation of the risk must be acted on before it impacts the project if at all possible. Not only that, any delay in reporting that is discovered later will lead to the question, "What were you waiting for? If you knew back then we could have . . ." You fill in the blank.

The most common example occurs in PC deployment projects. Unboxing, assembling, connecting, and firing up a computer on a network almost always include some logistics with existing equipment and desktop space. Even a thoroughly preconfigured computer still requires some minimal setup and configuration once it is placed. Invariably, an end user will ask the technician a question about the computer, its use, or other problems they may be experiencing.

The project planner can control the scope of the installation process by developing a script or sequence of tasks to be performed by the technician, including, all the tasks required to initialize the computer and connections. If additional time is not allocated in the resource and project duration estimates for user orientation and logistics, this type of scope creep can kill a project. Instead of spending 15 minutes hooking up a PC, the technician ends up spending an hour. Multiplied by 100 computers and the project goes from one week to four weeks. The PM can mitigate this by providing additional instructions for the technicians about what they can and can't do during the deployment.

Reports coming from the first day of deployment may trigger the risk assessment. If the original plan called for 15 minutes for each computer, and after the first day, the technicians report that installations are taking one hour because of a variety of reasons, the PM and project leads must then strategize on a modified or revised script, and a new deployment plan that allows the technicians to complete the installations in the allocated time, or the risk report must be triggered.

In this scenario, the risk report must state that installations are taking two to four times the original estimate. The mitigation actions might include:

1. Adding more technicians to the deployment team—additional resource cost
2. Revising the project completion date to a future date

There really is no option to stay on time without adding resources. This must be stated in the risk report.

The project would be well served to have a communication to the user community about the what, when, how, and whys of the upcoming deployment—part of the communications plan. This would be a good time to tell them to not interfere with the deployment team, not to ask them to set up printers and load additional apps, and to send additional service requests via the help desk or work order system.

Finally, instructions about "what if" the end user asks this or does not spend more than this much time could be added to the script in an effort to help control scope creep in the deployment project. The technician should have a prepared speech to address additional help or help them open a trouble ticket to request follow-up assistance.

Time Risk Factors

The example perfectly illustrates how scope creep also creates time risk factors, but there are many examples of when timing becomes a stand-alone risk factor. One is when a product delivery date is delayed because of availability or some other equipment acquisition delay. Because of these unforeseen delays, the PM is encouraged to include as many time considerations into the project plan. Adding a week of wait time or "acquisition delay" is a good way to account for gaps in the project timeline.

Past experience with product deliveries or knowledge from the manufacturer's sales representative about shipping lead times can bring more realism to the equipment acquisition time estimates. Also, adding time considerations or delays to estimates coming from SMEs will help expand a project timeline and provide allowances for delays out of the PM's control.

Sometimes large technology projects are hit with time risk factors and delays simply because of the size and scale of the project. When implementing one-to-one computers in schools, there may be no delays with device procurements in the hundreds or even thousands. But if your school decided to purchase 10,000 Chromebooks in June along with every other school in the country, suddenly a three-week delay may become a time risk.

These types of manufacturer's stock or product availability issues should be a key consideration not only during project planning but also in execution. Meaning that the manufacturer's sales representative may be a key SME for projects with lots of equipment. As part of the communications plan, the manufacturer's sales rep would be in the weekly meeting providing status for estimated equipment ship dates. The minute he or she starts off with a "Well, it sounds like there may be a product availability problem," your risk management plan should be triggered.

Budget Risk Factors

Budget risk factors obviously address cost. But cost may also be the constraint that is always directly or indirectly triggered by the other two: scope and time. It is most common to mitigate risks with additional resources to address the triple constraint – risk and resources = cost. Either by extension or by expansion, there is almost no way to mitigate risk factors without impacting budget. It is, however, a project planning skill, to build in enough time contingency and budget contingency into the project plan in anticipation of triple constraint risks.

For instance, in the classroom technology scenario, the PM may have included an additional day of integration labor for "cleaning up" after each classroom installation. This made up or anticipated scope contingency could easily save a project with some scope creep to keep within its time estimate and thereby helped mitigate a future project risk. Similarly, an extra budget for miscellaneous supplies could also keep the project cost within the overall project budget without triggering a risk assessment. Keeping in mind that too much contingency in project budgets can easily kill or limit the scope of a project beyond what is realistic or allowable.

The Risk Management Process

Figure 3.3—"Risk Management Process"—details the workflow for risk identification, assessment, reporting, and mitigation. It is noted that the first part of the process is to determine IF there is actually a project risk. It may be the case that something that seems like a project risk actually is covered by a contingency in the plan.

The initiating step for risk assessment is the receipt of new information or new data. This new information must be received, documented, analyzed, and assessed in regard to the three constraints: scope, time, and budget.

Once the potentially impacted constraints are determined, the PM must develop a high-level DRAFT risk assessment report. The DRAFT risk assessment is sent to the client to evaluate and decide if they approve of the risk assessment and acknowledge the risks. Why DRAFT you may ask? The risk assessment is presented as a DRAFT to give the client the opportunity to take action before publication of the risk assessment to other stakeholders outside the project—he or she is the client!

Upon client approval, the risk assessment report is published to all stakeholders.

The risk mitigation plan will address how the constraint issue will be dealt with and the project implementation plan will be revised. Typically, changes in scope will also trigger the change management process.

If the client does not approve of the DRAFT risk assessment report, it will be contingent on the PM to take one of the following actions:

- Revisit the constraint risks to see if anything can be done to mitigate any constraint impacts
- Revise the risk assessment to focus constraint impacts to different areas and resubmit
- Publish the report "as is" at the risk of getting removed from the project

Table 3.4—"Risk Assessment Table"—can be used to help define the project risks in developing the DRAFT and final risk assessment reports. Once the PM begins to define the risk type, it will likely come to light that two or all of the triple constraints may be affected by any new information, though

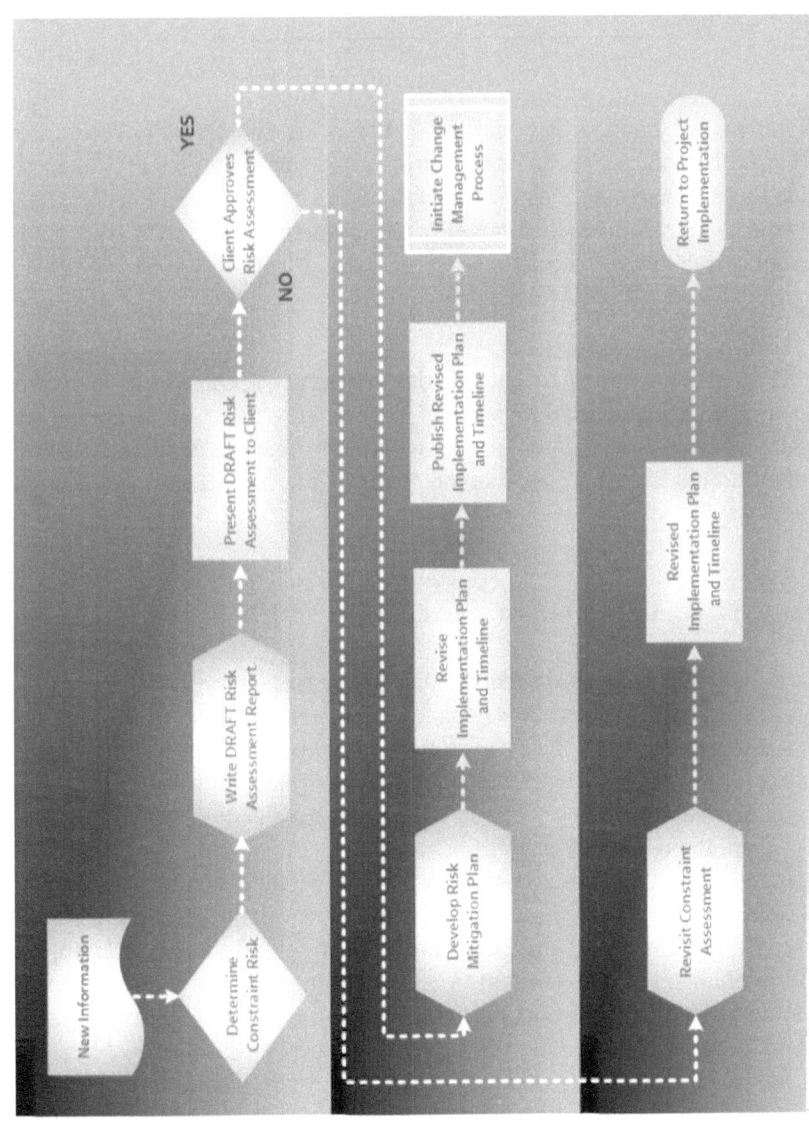

Figure 3.3 Risk Management Process

Table 3.4 Risk Assessment Table

Risk Type	Description	Implications	Mitigation
Scope			
Time			
Budget			

that is not always the case. It's possible that an equipment delivery delay may impact time but not scope or budget. But if additional actions are taken to mitigate the risk, these actions may actually trigger the change. For instance, hiring additional resources to complete a deployment will move the risk from a time delay to a budget increase.

PM Perspective

The PM must keep in mind that the risk assessment report is a device to trigger a change in the project success factors. If a piece of equipment is delayed, and additional budget is spent to expedite and get the equipment on time, then unless the client accepts the changes, the project may be deemed "over-budget."

CHANGE MANAGEMENT PLAN

In traditional ITIL parlance change management refers to projects in general, any project. In MAPIT® parlance change management refers to the support processes triggered when the project encounters a change before or during execution. This change is in reference to the initial plan that was developed in the planning phase of the project and typically triggered during a risk assessment or from the receipt of new information.

If triggered by a risk assessment report, that means that new information was received that was determined would impact one or more of the triple constraints. A risk mitigation would have been prepared and a REVISED implementation plan and timeline submitted to the client—not the entire group of stakeholders. That's because we want the client to be able to "make the call" on the risk determination. Upon acceptance of the risk mitigation plan, the triggering of change management processes are the revised implementation plans finally distributed to all stakeholders.

There is also a scenario where new information is provided that requires change management that didn't trigger a risk assessment. For instance, a shipping delay or equipment availability issue may have arisen that required an adjustment to project scheduling but didn't trigger a project risk because of contingencies in the plan. Or additional resources may have been necessary to replace or augment the team but all within the original constraints. So even though changes must be made and managed, they did not affect the overall project scope, time, or budget. Figure 3.4—"Change Management Process"—details how the change management process is triggered either by a risk mitigation report approved by the client, or directly through new information that did not trigger a risk assessment.

The PM must determine the constraint change elements—basically deciding which constraints are impacted by the risk mitigation or new information. The PM will then revise the implementation plan and submit the revised plan to the client for approval. Once approved, the revised implementation plan is published, and all resources and stakeholders are informed according to the communications plan.

Based on the change elements, the PM must identify the impacted resources and identify and obtain engagement vehicles. These are the contracting and confirmation methods used to engage the resources initially.

For instance, if a vendor is engaged to deploy all the switches in the Wi-Fi deployment, and now must extend the engagement for three weeks because of an equipment delay, then the PM must modify or amend the contract of services. This might be a simple reschedule of services that has no additional cost, or it might be a major project delay for that resource that may require new quotes, contracts, and budget to accommodate. The PM must recognize the bureaucracy that may arise in the middle of execution and have to drag new timelines and budgets back to leadership and financial decision makers.

The key to change management is the revision of the plan and the engagement or reengagement of resources. The change management process is key to keeping execution momentum going and to insure resources are engaged when they are needed. If there is new, different, or extra equipment required, if new resources or additional time is required, these types of new information will require change management. Whenever an original published plan is revised, it must be effectively communicated to all stakeholders in a timely manner. The more influential the stakeholder, the sooner he or she should be notified of a change in the implementation plan.

Because of the importance of this communication, the revision must be rock-solid and approved before setting out to redistribute it. There is nothing worse than issuing a revised timeline based on a preliminary judgment that is not final and causes a correction or another revision. Now the PM has multiple copies of the plan in circulation, and one of them will inevitably cause confusion to some. Although all stakeholders may be affected by the revision,

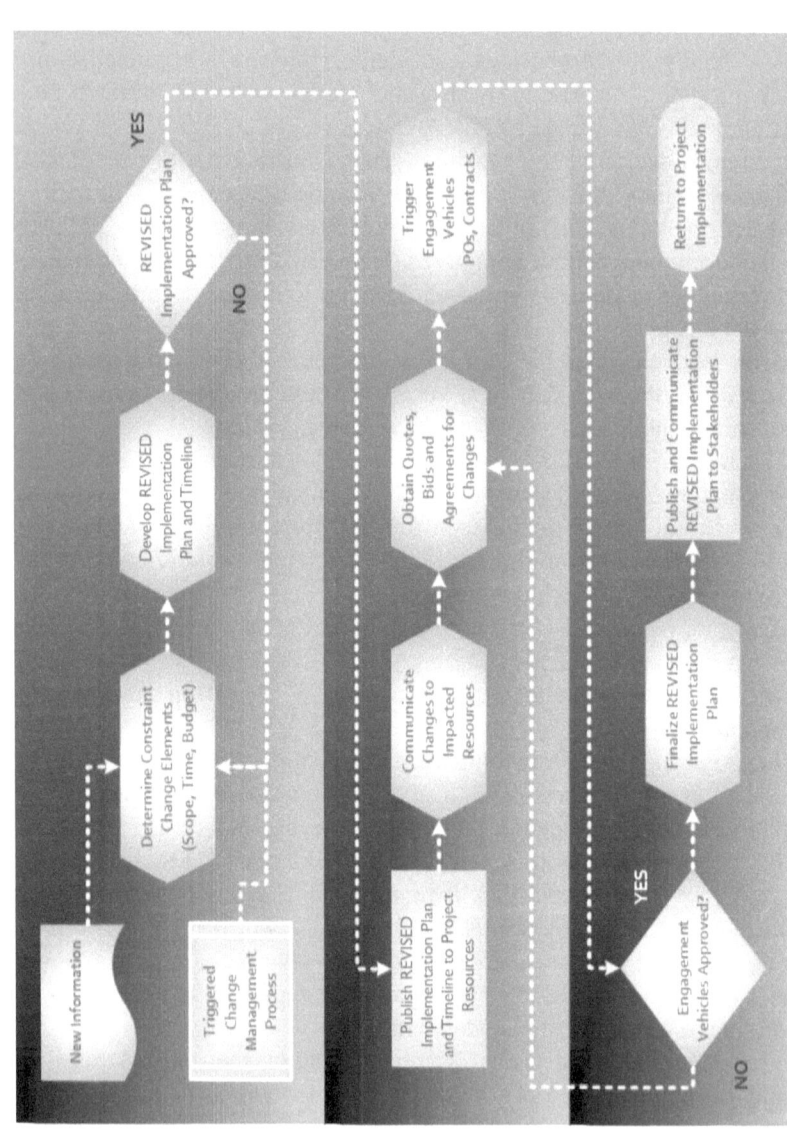

Figure 3.4 Change Management Process

the execution resources will have to adjust and revise their actual engagement times and durations, which may also impact cost. This is where engagement vehicles become top priority.

The change management process requires the PM to first notify all project resources of the proposed plan revision. Then the PM will communicate directly with impacted resources for new proposals, bids, quotes, and estimates for the changes. The operative components of the change management process are the engagement vehicles. The POs, contracts, or accepted proposals required to keep the project on the new schedule. Once these vehicles are initiated, then a finalized plan REVISION can be published to stakeholders.

If additional staff resources will be required, they will need to be estimated and requoted and likely new POs or contracts must be executed. Most service companies CANNOT schedule and commit resources without POs or signed contracts. They can't. In some cases getting a PO or contract signed could cause a gap in resource scheduling or equipment delivery. These unplanned gaps can cause huge cost overruns or missed timelines. What if a critical resource can't be rescheduled within the project window?

The PM cannot let administrative details, such as these, cause a project failure. Because of this criticality, the change management process holds back on publishing project plan revisions, until all changes are finalized and addressed, resources engaged, and POs signed. Then, and only then, the REVISED project plan can be published and distributed to all stakeholders.

QUALITY ASSURANCE PLAN

Quality assurance (QA) is the *process* of insuring that the correct methodologies and controls are in place during the project phases. For instance, just as the project controls help document and communicate progress and acceptance along the way, the QA plan identifies which instruments or documents will insure the highest quality of deliverable documenting and communicating each phase. QA is different from QC (quality control). QC refers to testing product outputs against metrics and overall workmanship. QA is part of each project phase whereas QC checks actual product.

QA actually starts along with the beginning of the project and is part of each of the project phases. In essence, the MAPIT® methodology *is* quality assurance. Figure 3.5—"Quality Assurance"—lists sample processes, documents or deliverables that may be used in the Quality Assurance Plan.

The MAPIT® quality assurance plan defines the instruments that will help insure the highest quality of output through effective use of the support processes and the methods to communicate and document the objectives and

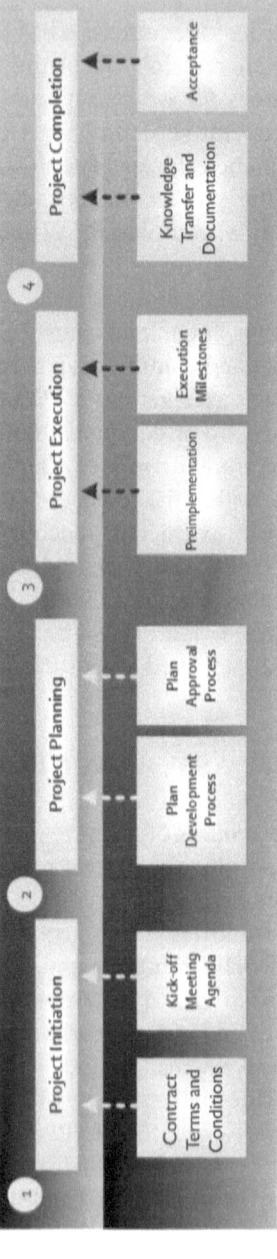

Figure 3.5 Quality Assurance

deliverables of each phase of the project. QA seeks to inject quality *controls* upon the inputs, and the processes and tasks of each phase, to insure quality outputs from each phase. In some cases these controls are manual tasks, such as following all the defined processes in plan development or performing the preconfiguration tasks during the execution phase. Others are actual devices, such as the signed terms and conditions and the customer acceptance, which may actually be final payment of invoices.

Contract terms and conditions are the formal legal document that memorializes and initiates any major project. The T&Cs allow both parties to come to a formal, legal understanding of the:

- date and expected timeline of the engagement;
- scope of work;
- responsibilities of each party;
- particulars of the relationship between the parties;
- methods of resolving disputes; and
- signatures of officers authorized to contractually obligate both parties.

Contract T&Cs are used to protect both parties in the agreement, but they are oftentimes avoided by small companies and service providers because they might require a legal review by the client's counsel, which in many cases may slow or even stop a project. From a QA standpoint, the T&Cs require that both parties agree on some very important legal details, so the contract T&Cs should always be used when engaging in any type of contracted technology implementation with services provided by a vendor.

The kick-off meeting is the formal activity that involves project stakeholders and provides the first major communication and call to action. The agenda defining the objectives of the kick-off meeting then becomes part of quality assurance. To fulfill that role, the kick-off meeting agenda must be more than introductions and project summaries. The kick-off meeting agenda should also be the platform to bring all stakeholders to the table and garner their trust in the planning and project management. A concise agenda will help foster that process. Review the Kick-off Meeting Agenda Template in chapter 1, table 1.4. If the PM truly covers all the items in this template, the kick-off meeting should be highly productive and support QA.

Through the planning process, a disciplined and structured approach during discovery and plan development is QA. Following tasks in sequence and identifying each milestone and metric will insure that each output is based on realistic input. Just using gross estimates and placeholders during the early planning processes can lead to gross errors in the execution phase. The PM must be disciplined about following logical sequential decision making in the planning process. Using tools such as MS Project to create a Gantt chart and then using the Gantt chart to aid in project status reporting and resource planning is a QA process.

Bypassing approvals upon completing the planning process is bypassing a QA process. If the PM is confident and ready to present a completed plan ready for execution, he or she should also be prepared to publish the plan to all resources and stakeholders and garner the appropriate approvals. The PM must fight the urge to jump right into execution without these approvals as this milestone might become suspect once a project risk is identified. "Who said to start the project when we knew I was going to be out of town?" said one dissatisfied client.

Through execution, the preimplementation tasks may be performance based as well as the execution milestones. In these cases, the project controls are in place to document weekly progress, and status reports should document the completion of execution milestones. In this respect the project controls are a component of the QA plan.

Finally the knowledge transfer (training) process and transfer of the systems documentation complete the QA process in the project completion phase, while the final acceptance document and final payment signify a true project completed and delivered. Other documents that can be part of the QA plan for any technology program may include:

- Final testing and verification
- AS-BUILT drawings
- Closeout

Table 3.5—"Quality Assurance Sample Template"—provides a sample of the instrument and type of output that can support total quality at each phase. It should be clear that each of the instruments utilized to support quality are also components of the final deliverable. Original scope of work, contract documents, and a solid agenda for the kick-off meeting help assure adherence to the original project objectives and clean contracts and agreements are in for project initiation.

Plans, timelines (Gantt charts), and project budgets are the outputs from a quality project planning process. Preimplementation processes define tasks; asset inventories and AS-BUILT documents provide value deliverables from the execution process. Systems documentation—both hard copy and electronic—along with the training plan and final acceptance document comprise the project completion. QA calls for the PM along with project resources and the client to review these documents at each phase of the project, not just at the end. Holding back these QA documents until the end negates the ability of the resources and client to review and ask for revisions at each step.

There's nothing worse than handing over the big binder of systems documentation at the end of the project and have the client say, "Where's the

Table 3.5 Quality Assurance Sample Template

Phase	Instrument	Type
Project initiation	Statement of work	Document
	Contract T&Cs	Contract
	Kick-off agenda	Agenda
Project planning	Core and Support Processes	Project plan
	SMEs	Time and resource estimates
	Designs and timelines	Diagrams and Gantt charts
	Plan approval	Plan funding
Project execution	Preconfiguration	Task
	Installation	Task
	Asset inventory	Inventory database
	Final configuration	AS-BUILT
Project completion	Punch list	Document
	Systems documentation	Hard copy and electronic
	Training schedule	Activity
	Customer acceptance	Document

inventory database? Fiscal is asking for it." If this wasn't specified and performed during execution, the PM has a big "make-good" task hanging out there.

DATA INTEGRITY PLAN

The idiom *garbage in, garbage out* is the moniker for data integrity. Data integrity has many flavors but has mostly come about with the development of database applications and data warehouses in the form of input processes and field constraints. Data integrity is different from data security in that data integrity defines processes to insure data is valid and correct. Data security defines methods and procedures to insure that data is secure from viruses, malware, bad actors, and competitors.

Within the context of educational technology projects, the MAPIT® data integrity plan attempts to identify data sources, both for planning and execution, and insure that the data is valid and accurate. It's not that there are viruses or bad actors targeting the project data, but poor data integrity can cause huge errors in planning and execution.

One of the most common forms of data corruption comes from the widespread use of spreadsheets. Although powerful for calculating, modeling, predicting, planning, and performing "what if" analysis, the spreadsheet is also powerful enough to sink a business or delay any project with just an inadvertent keystroke or undo. Using spreadsheets can be an occasion to inject invalid or inaccurate data into a process or project. Worse yet, complex table calculations and overused macros have also been the culprit in many a bad budget estimates.

But this also applies to the data provided in the planning processes that drive the implementation plans of technology projects. Any leeway on the integrity of data at the planning stages of a project will likely lead to errors, missed deadlines, or miscommunicated results at the end. Once again, garbage in, garbage out. If task estimates are not provided by the SME, or if obsolete tables were used to develop cost estimates, the data output has no chance of being accurate.

One common error in budgeting is using Internet searches to find street prices of components. Do a simple search for a Cisco router, and you may find routers ranging in cost from a few hundred dollars to several hundred thousand dollars. Equipment with additional memory or firmware might also reflect huge cost variances in products with very similar or even the same part number. Software products with additional modules or for different platforms can also cause variances in cost estimates. That's where the SME comes into play from a data integrity perspective.

If MAPIT® were a software development methodology, then this section might be half the book. Data integrity looks at all the data components of a technology project and seeks to implement controls over data types and ranges (states) and eliminate manual interactions and human error. The MAPIT® data integrity plan is process based; it seeks to identify areas where data is created, transferred, and maintained and to eliminate any human manual intervention. This eliminates keystroke errors, copy/paste errors, typos, duplication, and omission errors caused by people.

For instance, the purchasing agent is not the person to get the lead time for a new telecommunications circuit request—even though that person ordered the last one. This is an example of relying on invalid sources from a data integrity perspective. The real source of data for any type of telecommunications service should be the service provider only, not the rep, the consultant, or the techie. In one scenario, the last time a telecommunications circuit was ordered, it took 45 days. But if there might be any type of construction or "last mile" installation services, that circuit might take 90 days and include a $16,000 installation fee. That would be a big miss in project planning.

Another example is when different people are recording inventory lists from equipment packing lists, and they are typing in location information in nonstandard formats, like using all caps or using spaces where the standard is underscore or dash. Another example is entering names without consistent formatting, like using spaces between names like "de la Rosa" or the capitalization of nonleading letters like in "McCoy."

Once these spreadsheets are compiled, sorting and calculations will be as wrong as the inconsistent data. Similarly, in a software implementation project, such as a new student information system, the source of data

Support Processes

Table 3.6 Data Integrity Plan

Data	Source	Destination	Control
Structured cabling estimates	SME cabling contractor	Implementation plan	Use secondary source for cost and time estimates.
Network equipment cost estimates	Past procurements	ROM budget	Identify primary and secondary sources for manufacturer's discount and street price.
Student data for LMS	Student information system	LMS	Implement API for direct access to data.
Emergency contact information	Enrollment forms—online and manual	Student information system	Insure standard treatment of name conventions, e.g., McCoy, de la rosa, Higgs-Boson.
Telecommunications services cost and installation	Telecom services order analyst	Implementation plan	Initiate actual communications and preliminary orders through service provider.
Equipment shipping and delivery schedule	Reseller/integrator manufacturer's rep	Implementation plan and execution schedule	Request most recent availability and distribution through reseller.
Asset inventory	Equipment packing lists	Asset inventory	Use standard product names, part numbers, and serial numbers to be search and sortable.

coming from the legacy system would be a major component of the data integrity plan. The new system must be implemented without any of the data type and range errors that might exist in the legacy system. In this instance a process of data mining and cleansing may be required as part of the data migration process, once again injecting human intervention into the project.

The actual data integrity plan can take the form of table 3.6—"Data Integrity Plan."

PROJECT COMPLETION, ACCEPTANCE, DELIVERY, AND CLOSEOUT

Every project has a beginning, middle, and end. In MAPIT® parlance we can talk about (1) project initiation, (2) project planning, (3) project execution, and (4) project completion. In all cases, end/completion/closeout all mean the same thing—it's finished. Whether on time and on budget or not becomes a fact of history, but if significant delivery and final closeout are not achieved and accepted by the client, you can bet your project failed. If not in reality, likely in the minds of the client and stakeholders.

It's also possible that the PM thinks the project is a success and the client thinks otherwise, or vice versa. In any case, the best outcome is when all parties agree the project is completed and a success. The best indicator of project completion besides the instruments listed below is the receipt of final payment. It is possible to get this before getting the other final deliverables, but it is in the PM's best interest to produce all the deliverables defined in the project plan. Actions speak louder than words, and delivery of what was promised is a great milestone.

Breaking one or all of the triple constraints does not mean the project is a failure, as long as the client will sign off on acceptance and be a future reference. If the PM did everything possible to deliver a successful project on time and on budget, this is the determining factor for project success.

Project completion documents should have been defined in the project planning phase. Some of the documents may also be part of the communications plan, project control plan, QA plan, and the data integrity plan. The deliverables would likely include one or more of the following items:

- Final systems documentation and user manuals
- "AS-BUILT" drawings—hard copy and electronic
- Verification test results
- Punch list—Completed or significant completion
- The original RFP, scope of work, or contract document, addenda or extensions to the original contract
- Client acceptance

Final Systems Documentation and User Manuals

Depending on the project, systems documentation and/or user manuals may take different forms. It almost seems ridiculous these days to talk about hard-copy manuals, but there are still many times that this is appropriate. It's still a great sign of delivery when you hand over a three-ring binder and say, "Here's the complete systems documentation; it's also stored on your server in this folder."

Some of the most obvious components and documents that would be included in this binder include:

- The original RFP, scope of work, or contract document
- Research and data sheets from vendors of technology systems

- Bills of materials, quotes, proposals, and scopes of work from subcontractors
- Design diagrams
- Timelines (historical)
- As well as the following items

"AS-BUILT" Drawings—Hard Copy and Electronic

"AS-BUILT" drawings and CAD diagrams of actual work completed may be some of the most useful documents—yet hardest to obtain. Unless the PM included a certain specification of CAD drawings to be delivered with the systems documentation, there's a good chance the vendor will send some sloppy 8.5" × 11" Fire Exit maps with red line markups. This is not acceptable. The PM should be sure to include "AS-BUILT" CAD drawings of ARCH A–E sizes with single-line building plans and device or drop locations identified in RED to be delivered in hard copy along with the final deliverables. If the PM or client doesn't specify hard-copy deliverables, there's a chance that the vendor will say, "We sent it to you electronically, now you can print it any size you like." But you don't have an ARCH E size printer or plotter, do you? Printing of these large-scale drawings can become quite expensive, especially if there is one for each IDF closet at every school. Better specify it and don't sign off until it's delivered.

Verification Test Results

Another set of paper or electronic files that might never get looked at but must be part of the final deliverable are the verification testing results. Once again, these should have been specified as part of the scope of work, or else the extra work involved in exporting and organizing the test results may never be done or delivered.

However, these test results may be the evidence needed for future claims if the network or equipment is not performing up to specification. This is most important with structured cabling plants where fiber-optic backbone cabling and copper horizontal cabling become the core factor limiting overall network performance.

Fiber OM4 and Copper Category 6 cabling are being pushed to their operational limits supporting as much as 2, 8, and even 10Gbps. Any excessive lengths, bends, crimps, or poor terminations may result in poor network or Wi-Fi performance and diminished capacity under heavy network loads. These types of intermittent problems may be very difficult to troubleshoot and identify, but the verification tests for these network systems will show that they were performing to specification at the time of their delivery.

PMs can also develop their own customized verification tests for their projects such as some of the examples on table 3.7—"Performance Requirements

Table 3.7 Performance Requirements for Verification Testing

System	Performance Specification	Practical Verification
Copper horizontal cabling	– Category 6/up to 10Gbps	– 250Mhz
Fiber-optic backbone cabling	– Optical Multimode (OM) 4/up to 40Gbps	– 4,700MHz*km
Wi-Fi	– 802.11ac/1.3Gbps	– 100 Users @ 6.5Mbps
LMS	– Supports up to 10,000 users	– Two second minimum response time
ScreenCasting/sharing	– Wi-Fi, Wired, Bluetooth	– 33—Teachers and students

for Verification Testing". Including practical verification beyond the simple systems test will insure the vendor provide results of real-world testing of used and performance of applications as opposed to objective technology specs.

Punch List: Completed or Significant Completion

In any large-scale technology rollout or deployment project, there are always outstanding items known as the "punch list." Obviously items on this punch list are specific to the type of project, whether a Wi-Fi project or an LMS implementation. The punch list is the final list of must-do's for the vendor to get final sign-off, or what's known as "significant completion"—the level of acknowledged and accepted completion that would allow the vendor to send his or her final or penultimate invoice if the contract calls for a 5% to 10% holdback. This punch list with all the items checked off should be included with the final documentation.

Training Schedule

Every technology project or program will have training and/or knowledge transfer. These may be two different things, or a variety of things. Table 3.8—"Training and Knowledge Transfer"—provides examples of different types of training and knowledge transfer activities and the recipients or participants.

Client Acceptance

Possibly the second-most satisfying closeout process is the client acceptance letter (the most satisfying is the final payment). A short form letter providing all the relevant information and the project scope of work is used as a basis to gain client acceptance or significant completion. The form letter is submitted to the client for final acceptance and can be the trigger to issue the final invoice for payment. As a part of the closeout procedure and final project control, this document requires the client to sign off on the project scope of

Table 3.8 Training and Knowledge Transfer

Type	Form/Format	Participants
User training	Leader-led, lab training, train the trainer	Administrators and end users
Administrators' training	Hands on, one-on-one, on-the-job	System administrators
Knowledge transfer	Orientation, one-on-one, on-the-job	Administrators

work. And similar to the other support processes should be prepared before the actual project execution phase. This becomes an excellent last page of the systems documentation (before the appendices).

PROJECT EXECUTION

Once all the support processes are defined and published to the project team, then it is time to move on to project execution. This is where the rubber meets the road as they say. Once the project plan is presented, approved, and funded, project execution starts. This is the second-most important milestone of every project because if the planning is done correctly, execution should go smoothly.

It is suggested that the core processes are followed in sequence and flow in order to create an effective and useful project plan. The support processes must be defined and acknowledged as part of the project plan and subject to the same approvals before execution begins. If all goes well, the support processes will be only needed as reference—what to do if and when and how. But if the project plan is truly accurate and valid, only the communications plan will be in effect. No risks and no changes will signify successful planning. Accurate data inputs, outputs, and deliverables signify data integrity and quality assurance. Project control will signify milestones and project completion.

Now you're ready to execute. Ready, set, go!

Final Thoughts

This book detailed and explored the process of planning an educational technology project (core processes) and defining the processes that help assure project delivery (support processes). In the end it comes down to one thing—the project manager and this edict:

Project Management is the Project Manager

All these flowcharts, examples, and tables reinforce one point. Project management is a set of tasks and activities executed by a party responsible for project delivery by laying out plans, engaging resources, monitoring implementation, reporting progress, and delivering project deliverables according to objectives and projected timelines. The project manager must have the attitude and wherewithal to deal with personalities and foster a sense of teamwork, cohesion, shared sacrifice, and performance to objective. The project manager is coach, taskmaster, mentor, guide, and sheriff. His or her effort is to identify project objectives and advocate for the project over all objections, dissatisfaction, apathy, and even sabotage and subordination. The client relies on the PM to assure project delivery.

About the Author

Darryl Vidal has been involved with technology and education all his adult life. Starting in aerospace telecommunications, he worked as a systems engineer for Apple Computer in the late 1980s and began working directly with K–12 schools. By 1994, Darryl began providing technology consulting services to San Diego Unified School District and many other districts in the region, helping design and implement digital classrooms, wide area networks, VoIP, and wireless campuses. He holds a bachelor's degree in business and a master's in education technology.

For over 20 years, Darryl has been working at the forefront of education technology modernization programs from virtual classroom technology, through learning management systems helping plan and manage school technology upgrades totaling over $500,000,000.00.

Books by Darryl Vidal published by Rowman & Littlefield Publishing Group:

- *N3XT Practices: An Executive Guide for Education Decision Makers* (with Michael Casey)
- *VISION: The First Critical Step in Developing a Strategy for Education Technology* (with Michael Casey)
- *Confucius in the Technology Realm: A Philosophical Approach to Your School's Ed Tech Goals*
- *FAIL TO PLAN, PLAN TO FAIL: How to Create Your School's Education Technology Strategic Plan*

Other books by Darryl Vidal:

- *The Net Dude*: (a novel)
- *BACKSTAGE: Behind the Curtains with the Greatest Entertainers of the 20th Century*

www.ingramcontent.com/pod-product-compliance
Lightning Source LLC
Chambersburg PA
CBHW021847220426
43663CB00005B/430